Writing and Responding

a course for English language examinations

Chris Woodhead   with Ann Miller and Pat O'Shea

Oxford University Press

Oxford University Press, Walton Street, Oxford OX2 6DP

London   Glasgow   New York   Toronto
Delhi   Bombay   Calcutta   Madras   Karachi
Nairobi   Dar es Salaam   Cape Town
Kuala Lumpur   Singapore   Hong Kong   Tokyo
Melbourne   Auckland

and associate companies in
Beirut   Berlin   Ibadan   Mexico City

ISBN 0 19 831246 6

Photoset in Great Britain by
Rowland Phototypesetting Limited, Bury St Edmunds, Suffolk
and printed by Butler & Tanner Ltd.,
Frome and London

Preface

As you work through this book you will read a large number of passages which we have chosen to illustrate different kinds of writing. In choosing these passages we have kept the demands of the O level and 16 plus language examinations carefully in mind, and each chapter of the book will help you to improve your performance in these examinations. On finishing the book you should be able both to read and understand the different kinds of writing which you will meet in the examination and to cope effectively with any writing task which you might be set. We believe that the more you understand about how words can be used for different effects, the more you will appreciate the books which you read. We hope, therefore, that you will enjoy the passages which we have chosen, and that, in some cases at least, you will go on to read the book from which we have selected an extract. There is no doubt that the more reading you do, and the more you think about what you read, the better your own writing is likely to become.

Contents

Introduction

Essays and comprehension: some general advice

Most of the marks in O level and 16+ language examinations are reserved for two questions: the comprehension and the essay. So it is very important that you approach these questions in an intelligent and efficient way. This chapter gives advice about what each of these questions is designed to test, and about how you should set about answering them. It is best to read the chapter carefully before going on to study the more detailed advice in the rest of the book.

The essay

The first problem which you are faced with is choosing the title *which best suits your abilities*. There are basically two different types of essay which you might be asked to write: the imaginative and the practical. Later in this book you will be given detailed advice on how to approach each of these types of essay. What is important now is that you understand how they differ from each other in the demands which they make on the writer.

Imaginative writing

Consider the following list of questions:

1 Autumn comes like a plague,
   The bitter winds biting at the helpless leaves.
   They float, caught by the cruel wind,
   Then they die, their crumpled bodies scattered.
   The berries bright and glossy,
   Hang to keep each other warm, in bunches.
   The frost comes now crisp and fragile,
   Bringing freshness all around.
   Autumn is death – but what a death,
   Leaving multi-coloured leaves behind!
   New life will return with Spring.   *Beverly*

This is one girl's observations about Autumn.

Write a description of an autumn scene, stressing how different it is from other seasons.

2 Marathon.

3 You are baby-sitting and asked by two young children to make up a story. Write the story you tell them, making sure it is suitable for their age. It may be about fairies, animals or toys and may include the children for whom you are baby-sitting, but it must be original and not a story you have read or heard.

4 Childhood memories.

5 Write about ONE of the following:
- a) the operation,
- b) the christening,
- c) the bonfire,
- d) the street party.

Describe the atmosphere of the occasion and the feelings of the people involved. Do not merely tell a story.

6 Continue the following story, bringing out the characters of the various people involved.

The Concert

The week before Elsie Thomas had swept into my life. I, being thirteen and the youngest, kept aloof from the gang. Earlier Mildred Rogers had caught hold of my jacket, saying, "You go and join that lot around Elsie Thomas and I'll tell your Dad." My dad did not believe in girls.

I listened to the boastful chatter of the boys surrounding Elsie. The vicar clapped his hands.

"Take your seats please. Our concert is about to begin. Master Harry Smith is going to entertain us."

I stepped onto the stage.

"This will show them," I thought. "Wait until Elsie Thomas sees this!"

7 Study the photographs on the opposite page and write about them in any imaginative way you like.

Each of these questions asks you to create a scene or a story: to enter imaginatively into a particular situation so that you make that situation as vivid and as memorable to your reader as you can.

You will realize from studying these seven questions that there are at least three different types of imaginative writing:

☐ descriptive essays (as in questions number 1 and 5) where you are asked to evoke a particular scene.

☐ narrative essays (as in questions number 3 and 6) where you are asked to write a story.

☐ personal essays (as in question number 4) where you are asked to write in some way about yourself.

If you chose question 2 or 7 you could write either a descriptive essay or story.

Chapters One, Two and Three of this book will help you to write each of these types of imaginative essay. Try and develop the habit of studying essay titles in order to work out precisely what kind of writing they demand. You might then save yourself a great deal of time and wasted effort in the examination.

You will probably find as you work through the book that some kinds of essay appeal to you more than others. Which of these titles do you find most interesting? Select *one* and write an essay of about 400 words on it.

Practical writing

Now consider this second list of questions:

1 EXAMINATIONS

The comments printed below and the cartoon on page 11 are concerned with examinations or assessment. Study them and then discuss *some* of the points raised, adding points of your own in order to develop your arguments.

Father: "Julia stays in her room and emerges from time to time white-faced. She's under enormous pressure to get the right exam grades. Her job depends upon it."

Mother: "I've promised Steven a fiver for every O level he passes, but he spends all his time listening to pop. He says exams do not matter. His friend left at Easter and is already earning £50 a week. It wouldn't matter so much if Steven was a girl."

Patient: "I hope you've passed your exams, doctor!"

Headmaster: "Under continuous assessment there is knowledge not only of achievement but also of progress towards it. The syllabus and any final test necessary can be set by the teacher and so the motivation of the pupil is increased and tension and anxiety reduced. Pupils should always be assessed only on what they've been taught."

Headmistress: "One of the greatest dangers of allowing schools to set their own examinations is that teachers may be tempted to pass a child merely because he worked hard or to help him get a job. External examinations are completely impartial and are the best bulwark against poor standards."

Lecturer: "All that is needed is a school record, which states precisely what ground the pupil has covered, what projects he has done and exactly where he has succeeded and failed. Exams should be abolished altogether and the teachers allowed to develop school work that would genuinely engage the interest of all their pupils."

2 ADVERTISEMENTS

Write about your views on advertising. Refer to at least some of the points below, as well as, of course, adding points of your own which you think relevant.

Back up your discussion of the points raised by reference to the advertisements below and to any other advertisements, including those on television.

We've got Autoquip taped

Raven are the leaders in the field of car styling. Manufacturing self-adhesive decorative tapes for some of Europe's leading car manufacturers has given us a unique insight into the buying habits of today's style aware motorist.

hi·line CAR STRIPES
156 DIFFERENT COMBINATIONS OF COLOUR AND STYLE
SIMPLE TO FIT TO CAR, CARAVAN OR BOAT
SUPER TOUGH TAPES IN PERMANENT COLOURS
INSTANT DISTINCTIVE LUXURY LOOK FOR ANY CAR

Buy it from the people who make it

RAVEN ACCESSORIES
Manufacturers of Hi-line tapes
Apta House, Mesnes Green, Cherry Orchard, Lichfield.
Telephone: 05432-55251. Telex: 336046

For:

Advertisements encourage the buying of new products; without them new products would not stand a chance. Without them we would not be able to decide which is the best buy. They create a diversity of taste; their colourful designs and witty slogans often add a bit of spice into a grey, drab world. Besides advertisements increase sales and therefore lower prices.

Against:

Some advertisements are an insult to our intelligence. Many, however, subtly exploit our fears and play upon our emotions, particularly those associated with a particular age or class. They often appeal to our day-dreams and create false hopes. Some try to hoodwink us by use of pseudo-scientific jargon. Many help to perpetuate the rat-race for material possessions.

13

3 Read the following article written by a vicar in a parish magazine and then write a letter to him, stating how far you agree or disagree with some at least of his views. Add any points of your own which you think help to develop your argument.

St. Andrew's Vicarage,
Northport.

"In an ideal society, everybody would be paid the same", said an M.P. recently, "but in the world as it is, some people inevitably have to be paid more than others."

So far most people, I suppose, agree. Certainly some people need more money to do their jobs properly. Others have to work awkward hours or in dangerous conditions. They too deserve special allowances.

But the M.P. went on to say that the position of influence and responsibility occupied by M.P.s should be reflected in their pay.

But who has the most influence? People in the public eye frequently have less influence than those who work behind the scenes.

Who has the most responsibility? Some workers have even gone on strike to prove to others just how much responsibility their job entails!

There is a lot to be said for paying people as human beings responsible to God, and, except for the special circumstances mentioned earlier, eliminating all differentials.

For whom do we value most? A cabinet minister, a company director, a trades-union leader, a pop star, an Olympic gold medallist?

Wilberforce Wright

Answering any of these questions would involve you in writing a practical essay. A practical essay is one in which you have to organize a number of facts or articulate an opinion. It calls not so much for imagination as for the ability to structure your material so that the reader can follow and understand each stage in your account or argument.

Further advice on this type of writing is given in Chapter Four. At this stage simply learn to recognize the essay questions which involve these kinds of skills.

For practice, answer one of the above three questions. Write for about 45 minutes, which is the time you would be allowed in the examination.

- ☐ Think before you write. Think about the kind of writing skills each essay title demands, and, if you have the choice, choose that essay which suits your abilities best.

- ☐ Think, too, about what kind of experience or knowledge is needed to write convincingly about a particular topic. People write best about what they know something about, so, if you can, select a title which allows you to draw upon your own experience.

- ☐ Don't panic! Time spent thinking is time well spent.

Comprehension exercises

This exercise is a test of whether you can understand a piece of writing and express this understanding in a clear and concise fashion. Depending on the examination board which you sit, you may find that the passage set for comprehension is either an 'imaginative' or a 'practical' piece of writing. Several boards set two comprehension exercises, one on an imaginative passage and another on a practical one.

Whatever the type of passage, always follow this set procedure in tackling comprehension exercises.

1 Read the passage through fairly quickly to gain a general impression of what it is about.

2 Read it through a second time slowly and carefully *before* starting to answer any questions.

3 Read the questions equally carefully, so that you are certain that you know exactly what each question is trying to find out. Far too many candidates misunderstand questions and therefore provide answers which are wrong or irrelevant.

4 When you feel that you have a firm grasp of both the passage and the question, you are in a position to start writing. When you have written an answer to a question re-read the actual question to check that your answer is, in fact, relevant.

5 Always answer in your own words unless you are specifically asked to quote from the passage: the point of a comprehension exercise is to test your understanding of the original passage, and if you quote words and phrases from the original you are not giving the examiner evidence of this understanding.

6 Always write in complete sentences unless you are specifically told that you may answer with a single word or phrase. This is not just a meaningless ritual: part of the point of the exercise is for you to prove that you can express yourself clearly and coherently.

7 Do not introduce personal opinions (unless asked for them) or new information.

8 Some examination boards tell you the marks which are allocated to each question. This is to help you decide how long your answers ought to be. The more marks which are allocated to the question, the more detailed your answer should be.

Now try the following comprehension exercises. Each is taken from an actual examination paper. The first is an imaginative and the second a practical piece of writing. The second exercise is an example of a multiple-choice comprehension test. It demands exactly the same kind of approach as the traditional test. Be sure, however, to consider each alternative *carefully* before deciding which is the most likely answer to the question.

Blackmail

('The Jackal', an international assassin, collects a forged driving licence from a Belgian photographer, who attempts to blackmail him.)

"Very good," the Jackal said coolly. "Just what I wanted. I congratulate you. There is fifty pounds outstanding I believe."

"That is true, Monsieur. Merci." The forger waited expectantly, kneading his fingers together and with faint beads of sweat breaking
5 out on his forehead.

The Englishman drew a single wad of ten five-pound notes from his pocket and handed them over but before he let go of the wad, that he held between forefinger and thumb, he said, "I believe there is something more, no?"

10 The Belgian tried unsuccessfully to look as if he did not comprehend.

"Monsieur?"

"The genuine front page of the driving licence. The one I said I wanted back."

15 There could be no doubt now that the forger was playing theatre. He raised his eyebrows in extravagant surprise, as if the thought had just occurred to him, let go of the wad of bills, and turned away. He walked several paces one way, head bowed as if deep in thought, hands held behind his back. Then he turned and walked back.

20 "I thought we might be able to have a little chat about that piece of paper, Monsieur."

"Yes?" The Jackal's tone gave nothing away. It was flat, without

16

expression apart from a slight interrogative. The face said nothing either, and the eyes seemed half shrouded, as if they stared only into
25 their own private world.

"The fact is, Monsieur, that the original front page of the driving licence with, I imagine, your real name on it, is not here. Oh, please, please . . . ," he made an elaborate gesture as if to reassure one seized by anxiety, which the Englishman gave no sense of being . . . ,
30 "it is in a very safe place. In a private deed box in a Bank, which can be opened by no-one but me. You see, Monsieur, a man in my precarious line of business has to take precautions, take out, if you like, some form of insurance."

"What do you want?"

35 "Now, my dear sir, I had hoped that you might be prepared to do business on the basis of an exchange of ownership of that piece of paper, business based on a sum somewhat above the last figure of a hundred and fifty pounds which we mentioned in this room."

40 The Englishman sighed softly, as if slightly puzzled by the ability of man to complicate unnecessarily his own existence on this earth. He gave no other sign that the proposal of the Belgian interested him.

"You are interested?" asked the forger coyly. He was playing his part as if he had rehearsed it at length; the oblique approach, the
45 supposedly subtle hints. It reminded the man in front of him of a bad old film.

"I have met blackmailers before," said the Englishman, not an accusation, just a flat statement in a flat voice.

The Belgian was shocked.

"Ah, Monsieur, I beg you. Blackmail? That is the pursuit of
50 scoundrels. What I propose is not blackmail since that is a process that repeats itself. I propose simply a trade – the licence for a certain sum of money."

Answer the questions in YOUR OWN WORDS unless you are asked to give a quotation.

The marks available for each question are shown in the brackets to help you decide the length of your answers.

a) What emotions are shown by the forger while he "waited expectantly"? (lines 3–5) (2)

b) What does the author mean when he describes the forger as "playing theatre"? (line 15) (2)

c) What does the forger mean by his "precarious line of business"? (lines 31–2) (2)

d) What did the forger do which made the Jackal think of him
   as a character in "a bad old film"? (lines 45–46) (4)

e) Explain the forger's argument that he is not a blackmailer.
   (lines 49–52) (4)

f) i) List THREE characteristics which describe the attitude
      of the Jackal in the passage.

   ii) Illustrate each characteristic you have listed with a
       QUOTATION from the passage. (6)

Read the following passage carefully and then answer Questions **1** to
25 which are connected with it.

In animals, misery can result from two causes only – restraint and
disease; consequently, animals in a state of nature are never miserable. They are not hindered or held back. Whether the animal is
migrating or hibernating, or flying from some ferocious enemy which
5 may perhaps kill him, or courting, or incubating over long periods, or
fighting, he is obeying the impulse that is strongest in him at the
time – he is doing what he wants to do, the one thing that makes him
happy.

Disease is so rare in wild animals, or so quickly proves fatal, that
10 compared with disease in human beings, it is practically non-
existent. The disease either kills so quickly or is so quickly outlived
that the pain is brief and cannot be called misery. Inevitably, most
wild animals experience moments of fear but these moments vanish
when whatever excited them has passed, as the shadow of a summer
15 cloud vanishes when the cloud passes. When death comes it is unexpected and is not the death that we think of, with fear, all our lives,
but a sudden blow that takes away consciousness – the touch of
something that numbs the nerves – the prick of a needle. Whether the
animal dies by violence or excessive cold, his death is a compara-
20 tively easy one. While he is fighting or struggling to escape from an
enemy, wounds are not felt and scarcely hurt him. The same is true of
men, as many know from their own experience. When caught, if
death is not practically instantaneous, the disabling blow is itself a
kind of drug, producing insensibility to pain. This, too, is a matter of
25 human experience. Many men have been fearfully lacerated by
savage beasts and have lived to tell of this strange numbness. Even
when they saw and knew that the animal was tearing their flesh, they
seemed not to feel it, and were at the time not concerned about their
fate.

30 It is the same in death from cold. A strong man, lost in the Arctic
wastes, may experience some exceedingly bitter moments before he
gives up the struggle to live. The physical pain is simply nothing; the

18

whole bitterness is in the thought that he must die, leaving those he
loves and his dreams of the future; and compared to this, the creep-
35 ing coldness in his blood is nothing more than a slight discomfort.
Soon he is overcome by drowsiness and ceases to struggle; his only
thought is to lie down and sleep. And when he gives way to sleep, he
dies – very easily, very painlessly.

The bird, however hard the frost, flies briskly to his usual
40 roosting-place and falls asleep. He has no fears; only the warm blood
grows colder and colder, the pulse feebler and feebler as he sleeps,
and at midnight or in the early morning, he drops from his perch –
dead. Yesterday, he lived and moved, flying with marvellous certi-
tude and delicate precision; today, he falls from your hand like a
45 stone. But he was never miserable.

Each of Questions **1** to **25** is followed by five possible answers
lettered **A** to **E**. Select the best answer to each question and write its
letter down.

1   'Animals in a state of nature' as used in line 2 refers to animals that
are

   A in a safari park.

   B without artificial protection.

   C domesticated but untrained.

   D healthy and well-fed.

   E free from the influence of men.

2   According to the first paragraph, all of the following make an animal
happy EXCEPT

   A endangering his life by migration.

   B sitting for long periods hatching eggs.

   C risking injury fighting for a mate.

   D running in fear from a powerful predator.

   E being prevented from following his instincts.

3   Which combination of the following comes nearest to indicating fully
the subject-matter of the first paragraph?

   1 The various natural activities of wild animals.

   2 Wild animals are happy when obeying their instincts.

   3 The two possible reasons for unhappiness in animals.

   4 The instincts of wild animals can cause suffering.

   5 Restriction of animals is unjustifiable.

Turn over for rest of question

A 1 and 3 only

B 2 and 4 only

C 2 and 3 only

D 3 and 4 only

E 1 and 5 only

4 Which of the following reasons for disease among animals being 'practically non-existent' (lines 10–11) are given in the passage?

1 Many sufferers soon die.

2 Animals have a natural immunity to disease.

3 Wild animals are not overcrowded.

4 Their outdoor life keeps them healthy.

5 Unless the disease kills, the animal soon recovers.

A 2 and 4 only

B 1 and 3 only

C 1 and 5 only

D 4 and 5 only

E 2 and 5 only

5 According to the passage, pain in animals differs from misery because it is

A more disabling.

B physical rather than mental.

C more agonising.

D less lasting.

E less common.

6 Which ONE of the following words is closest in meaning to 'inevitably' as used in line 12

A assuredly

B unavoidably

C unsurprisingly

D probably

E certainly

7 Which ONE of the following words is closest in meaning to 'excited' as used in line 14?

A pleased

B over-joyed

C aroused

D inflamed

E exasperated

8 'As the shadow of a summer cloud vanishes when the cloud passes' (lines 14 and 15) illustrates that animals

    A are happiest when the sun shines.

    B fear moving shadows.

    C are always aware of changes in the weather.

    D sometimes feel fear without good reason.

    E feel fear only when the cause of it is present.

9 The passage argues that animals are not frightened of death for which one of the following reasons?

    A They are unaware of the possibility of death.

    B They recognise death as natural.

    C They realise its inevitability.

    D They do not have responsibilities to others.

    E They are completely self-centred.

10 Which ONE of the following words is closest in meaning to 'consciousness' as used in line 17?

    A liveliness

    B feelings

    C perception

    D wakefulness

    E awareness

11 Which ONE of the following is implied by 'the prick of a needle' as used in line 18?

    A an anaesthetic injection

    B the sharp claws of an enemy

    C an almost invisible injury

    D a slight but dangerous wound

    E a mortal stab

12 Which of the following possible reasons for an animal's death are NOT covered in the passage?

1 climate

2 accident

3 malnutrition

4 illness

5 old age

A 1, 2 and 3 only

B 2, 3 and 5 only

C 1 and 4 only

D 1 and 2 only

E 2, 4 and 5 only

13 Which ONE of the following is used as evidence to support the writer's argument that an animal's wounds are not felt during fighting?

A Men have reported similar freedom from pain.

B An animal's nervous system is insensitive to pain.

C Animals express anger but not pain when struggling.

D Animals give up when overpowered.

E Concentration on fighting prevents awareness of pain.

14 Which ONE of the following words is closest in meaning to 'fate' as used in line 29?

A fears

B sufferings

C misfortunes

D doom

E tragedy

15 Which ONE of the following statements about death from cold is meant by 'It is the same' as used in line 30?

A Men and animals are equally liable to it.

B It is scarcely felt by men and animals.

C It is similar to any other death.

D It is more common in animals than men.

E Men and animals have the same attitude to it.

16 Which ONE of the following comes nearest to indicating fully the subject-matter of the third paragraph?

   A death of a strong man

   B the approach of death

   C how a man dies from cold

   D a slow but painless death

   E dying in one's sleep

17 Which ONE of the following comes nearest to indicating fully the subject-matter of the fourth paragraph?

   A the gradual approach of death to a bird

   B a bird's painless death from cold

   C a bird has no fear of death

   D a bird dies without misery

   E a bird's death in the night

18 Which ONE of the following is closest in meaning to 'creeping' as used in lines 34–35?

   A spreading slowly

   B increasing irregularly

   C approaching carefully

   D arriving imperceptibly

   E invading dangerously

19 Which of the following statements are implied about the bird by the use of the word 'briskly' in line 39?

   1 He is vigorous and energetic.

   2 He feels cold and is trying to keep warm.

   3 He feels unwell and wishes to sleep.

   4 He feels healthy and is unworried.

   5 He is happy to die on his usual perch.

   A 1 and 4 only

   B 2 and 3 only

   C 3 and 4 only

   D 2 and 4 only

   E 2 and 5 only

20 Which ONE of the following words is closest in meaning to 'precision' as used in line 44?

A confidence

B awareness

C exactness

D sharpness

E alertness

21 The main purpose of the sentence beginning 'Yesterday, he lived' and ending 'like a stone' (lines 43–5) is to

A describe a bird's flight.

B show the sharpness of the frost.

C show the bird had no time to be unhappy.

D express admiration for the bird's skill in flight.

E express pity for the bird's death.

22 A man dying from cold differs from a bird dying from cold in all of the following ways EXCEPT

A his bodily suffering is slight.

B he struggles to stay alive.

C he is aware of the approach of death.

D his thoughts are for his family.

E his mental suffering is bitter.

23 The passage gives all of the following reasons for believing a wild animal is not made miserable by violence EXCEPT

A while fighting he does not feel wounds.

B death from violence is almost instantaneous.

C his enemy's blows make him unaware of pain.

D he is too frightened to be miserable.

E while fighting he is not worried whether he lives or dies.

24 According to the passage, which ONE of the following can cause misery to animals?

A momentary pain

B restriction of activities

C excessive cold

D fear of other animals

E the thought of death

25 Which ONE of the following comes nearest to indicating the theme of the whole passage?

   A Wild animals die easily.

   B A comparison of human death and animal death.

   C Death from disease among animals is rare.

   D Death from cold is almost painless.

   E Wild animals are never miserable.

These essays and comprehension exercises have been taken from actual examination papers. The examination boards vary slightly in the demands which they make, but you should now have a general understanding of the kinds of question you will have to answer. Go back at this point and re-read the essay titles and comprehension exercises. Think about your answers, and, in particular, about anything which you found difficult. Develop, in other words an alert approach to what you are doing, and keep a sense of your own strengths and weaknesses in mind as you work through the following chapters.

Chapter One

Descriptive writing

In this chapter you will learn about the different ways in which it is possible to describe experiences and places. You will appreciate from the introduction how necessary it is to understand how writers can capture something of the real world in their descriptions. If you choose to write a story in the essay section of the examination then almost inevitably you will have to include descriptive passages. Some essay titles ask you quite directly to describe something. It is possible, moreover, that you will be asked in a comprehension exercise to explain how the writer has built up his or her descriptive effects. This, then, is an important chapter which will repay careful study.

Different ways of describing the same place

You might think that if it is a place which is being described – your home town, for instance – then any one account is going to be much like any other. The photographs and passages printed below show that this is far from true. How someone describes a place depends on the purpose of their description, and, in some cases, upon their attitude to the place. Study these photographs of Brighton.

☐ What aspect of Brighton does each photograph show?
Where might you expect to find each photograph?

Each of the following passages is about London. The questions that follow will help you to understand each piece, and to appreciate what exactly the writer is doing.

London is the capital and largest city of the United Kingdom. The city (coterminous with the county of Greater London) covers 1580 km (610 mi) and has a population of 7,030,000 (1976 est.). The first settlement, the Roman Londinium, was founded in AD43 on a terrace near the north bank of the River Thames, 64 km (10 mi) from its estuary in the North Sea. The river is tidal, and London has been a port for seagoing vessels since the Roman period. London's size and population mirror the city's economic importance; it is one of the world's leading financial and insurance centres, as well as an important industrial city.

London's climate is one of mild winters, with an average temperature of 6° C (43° F) in January; summers are cool with a July average temperature of 18° C (64° F). The average rainfall is 585mm (24ins.) and is heaviest in October and November. The city has a reputation for severe fog as a result of the damp air combined with atmospheric pollution. The pollution has, however, been much reduced in recent years.

The Macmillan Family Encyclopaedia

1 This description is largely factual. What different *kinds* of fact do we learn about London?

2 How would you describe the way in which these two paragraphs are written?

3 Are there any descriptive words used which communicate anything of the atmosphere or character of the city? If so, what are they? If you do not think that there are any, why is this the case?

4 Would writing like this be appropriate in a letter written to a friend, or in a story? Give reasons for your answer.

This second passage is taken from a tourist brochure printed by the British Tourist Authority. It, too, contains a fair amount of information. As you read it, ask yourself, however, how the style of this passage differs from that of the first.

Take steps in the right direction to lead you to all the famous sights, sounds, splendid spectacles, shops and services available – all part of the bustling, busy and exciting city of London. A city that welcomes everybody and enjoys playing host to visitors from all over the world. A city that offers entertainment, cultural interest, rich pageantry, historic treasures, world-renowned landmarks and up-to-date facilities for the modern tourist. A vast metropolis – unique in character – where bells ring out the famous 'Oranges and Lemons' of the nursery rhyme; where the Household Cavalry may be seen, their shining helmets bedecked with plumes that swing and wave as they trot on sleek, perfectly matched horses, along the Mall. And always on hand to guide you, are 'the men in blue' – our friendly 'Bobbies' – the backbone of our police. It's an exciting year for London's Metropolitan Police Force which will be celebrating its 150th Anniversary (1829–1979). There are the familiar landmarks of Nelson's Column, Big Ben and the Tower of London. But perhaps more than anything the scarlet double-decker buses conjure up the London scene. And 1979 celebrates '150 Years of London Buses'. The first omnibus was horse-drawn and appeared on the streets of London in 1829. A link with the horse bus days of the 1830s will be provided during 1979 when a number of London Transport Routemasters in green and yellow livery run in public service in Central London to commemorate 150 years of the London bus.

London's first omnibuses, drawn by horses, were operated by a London coachbuilder, George Shillibeer, between Paddington and the Bank. The service began on July 4, 1829, with a fare of one shilling.

Digging up the past is always an adventure and in London you have many opportunities to unearth historic facts and discover links between the past and the present. It is self-evident that London (a site of little importance before the Roman conquest) owes its existence and prosperity to its port. In the 12th century it was already assuming a leading role among European trading centres. In the 14th and 15th centuries London was the headquarters of the wool trade. Then the city began to spread, and ensuing centuries left a heritage of landmarks familiar to us today – from St. Paul's Cathedral to the elegant squares and terraces of the 18th and early 19th centuries. The Victorian era brought years of unprecedented prosperity which have left their imprint in the shape of magnificent buildings and monuments.

Let it be said that modern development has made many changes in this city's skyline – but quickly add that the old, the elegant and the classical are still to be found here, to be enjoyed alike by citizens and visitors. And one of London's greatest attractions are the wide open spaces where building is not permitted – and the delightful Royal Parks – havens of tranquil peace amidst the hub and throb of a thriving city.

British Tourist Authority 1979

1 How is the style of the first sentence different from that of the encyclopaedia entry?

2 What is the writer of this passage trying to achieve, and why would his language be inappropriate in an encyclopaedia?

3 The only precise information which is given in this passage has to do with the fact that the Metropolitan Police and London Transport were both celebrating anniversaries in 1979. Why does the writer choose to give this particular information?

4 Does this passage tell you any more about what it is like to live in London than the encyclopaedia entry? Give reasons for your answer.

This third view of London is a much more personal description. The writer, Jonathan Raban, does not set out to communicate information about London. Neither does he want to persuade you that you might like to visit the city for a holiday. His aim is rather to suggest to you how London seemed to him when he first came to live there.

When I came to London, I took a room in a friend's flat in Highgate, a few steps from the spectacular wrought-iron Arch-way Bridge which carries a sedate Edwardian avenue high over the ravine of the A1. Up on the crest of the hill, one is in the world
5   of the forever fading glory of sober, middle-class prosperity. Down in the thick chemical air of the ravine, one is in the quick-penny land of used-car dealers, betting shops, grave Irish bar-loungers, and men who stop you in the street with offers of second-hand shirts. I lived for a few months midway between the
10   two; it was perfect territory for an immigrant, a place at once inside and out of the city, a hill with a view.
        From Archway Bridge, London in summer looks like a primi-tive lake-city on stilts; only the top storeys of the new tower blocks stick out from the turquoise mirror of exhaust fumes –
15   the pre-1960 city, in which St Paul's was the dominant architec-tural landmark, is completely submerged. Human life down there is mysterious, subaqueous; the traffic disappears down into the blue, rippling and steaming as it goes. It was from this hill that Whittington turned again (a pub and a milestone mark the spot),
20   and a mile to the west Guy Fawkes's fellow conspirators sat it out on Parliament Hill Fields, waiting for the brilliant splash on the sky that never came. They must have seen it in their heads again and again, painfully slow, a dream sequence in a movie cranked at half speed. The city itself is a mirage from here: one
25   might see or hear anything – promises, revolutions, ancestral phantoms – in that immense, ambiguous ripple of population and power.

Jonathan Raban   *Soft City* 1974

1 Using your own words explain the meaning of the phrase Jonathan Raban uses to describe Highgate: 'the world of the forever fading glory of sober, middle-class prosperity'. (line 5)

2 In the sentence which begins 'Down in the thick chemical air of the ravine . . .' (line 6) Raban pinpoints his impression of the London which stretches out beneath Highgate Hill.

   Why do you think he uses the word 'ravine'?

   In a sentence of no more than 25 words summarize Raban's de-scription.

3 Why (lines 12–13) does London look like 'a primitive lake-city on stilts'?

4 The last sentence in this passage is interesting because of the complexity of Raban's attitude towards the city he is describing. How would *you* describe his feelings as he looks down on London?

You have now read three very different descriptions of London. The first was baldly factual, the second deliberately persuasive, the third personal and atmospheric. There is no point in trying to decide which is the 'best' description, for each passage has a different purpose. The lesson to learn from thinking about these three passages is rather that before writing a descriptive essay of your own you need to have a clear sense of what you want your essay to achieve.

Do you want it to convey information? Or to make the reader react in a particular way? Or do you want to define your own *personal* attitude to what it is you are describing? Or what?

The point is that you must decide *what* it is you want to do before you begin. Then you must think about *how* best to do it.

Re-read the three passages. Think about how they differ in their language and style, and try to remember the wide range of options open to you in your own writing.

Your own writing

☐ Using the three passages which you have just read as examples, write a description of a town or country district you know well in the style of:

   a) an encyclopaedia entry

   b) a tourist article

   c) an imaginative account which tries to capture the essential atmosphere of the place you are writing about.

In order to write descriptions (a) and (b) you will probably have to go to the library to find relevant information. Make a list of the facts you discover, and decide which of these facts you are going to use in each description *before* you start writing.

Evoking atmosphere

These descriptions all attempt to capture the essential atmosphere of the place which the writer is describing. They resemble, therefore, the passage by Jonathan Raban (above) rather than the entry from the encyclopaedia or the tourist article. The questions which follow each passage are intended to help you understand something of how the writer has created the impression which he wants to communicate to his readers. Your own descriptive writing will certainly improve if you become more aware of the techniques which you can use.

The writer of the first poem, T. S. Eliot, is describing a city scene. (At the time when the poem was written, steak was not the luxury meat that it is now.)

Preludes

> The winter evening settles down
> With smell of steaks in passageways.
> Six o'clock.
> The burnt-out ends of smoky days.
> 5   And now a gusty shower wraps
> The grimy scraps
> Of withered leaves about your feet
> And newspapers from vacant lots;
> The showers beat
> 10 On broken blinds and chimney-pots,
> And at the corner of the street
> A lonely cab-horse steams and stamps.
> And then the lighting of the lamps.

T. S. Eliot 1917

1 Write down all the adjectives used in the poem. They have clearly been chosen with great care. What impression do they create?

2 The cab horse and the observer are the only living things in the poem. Why do you think Eliot has not included any human faces or voices in the poem?

3 If you had to read the poem aloud, how would you read line 3?

4 What do you take line 4 to mean? Are the 'smoky days' compared to anything?

5 In no more than 75 of your own words summarize the impression of city life which this poem creates.

This second poem is also about a city at night.

Late night walk down Terry Street

A policeman on a low-powered motorcycle stops.
His radio crackles, his helmet yellows.

Empty buses heading for the depot
Rush past the open end of Terry Street.

5   In their light, a man with a bike walking home,
Too drunk to ride it, turns into Terry Street.

Taxis swerve down Terry Street's shortcut,
Down uneven halls of Street Lighting Department yellow.

Into which now comes the man with the bike,
10   Struggling to keep on his legs.

The policeman waits under a gone-out streetlamp.
He stops the drunk, they talk, they laugh together.

I pass them then, beside dark, quiet houses,
In others mumbling sounds of entertainment;

15   Cathode-glows through curtains, faint latest tunes;
Creaking of bedsprings, lights going out.

Douglas Dunn   *Terry Street* 1969

1   Why does Dunn bother to state that the policeman's motorcycle is 'low-powered' (line 1)?

2   Why does his helmet 'yellow' (line 2)?

3   Why (line 4) does Dunn use the word 'rush' rather than, say, 'go' or 'drive'?

4   What is the effect of the last two verses?

5   This poem, unlike T. S. Eliot's poem, is full of human activity. What effect does this fact have on the impression which Dunn creates of city life?

The next example is from a novel but you will again note how the use of carefully chosen details explains much of the impact which the description has.

He walks along the terrace, with its cracked pavement stones, its scatter of broken glass; the rain soaks his hair, and begins to stipple the leather of his coat. The terrace curves around him; once an exact and elegant half-circle, the curious dentistry of
5   demolition has attacked it, pulling out house after house from the curve as they have become empty. Most of those that still stand are unoccupied, with broken roofs and vacant, part-boarded windows, plastered with posters for political parties, pop groups, transcendental meditators, or rather surreptitiously

10 occupied, for they are visited by a strange, secret, drifting population of transients. But, though there are few residents, the
terrace has been metered for parking; the Kirks have to keep their
minivan some streets away, in a square up the hill. A police car
heehaws on the urban motorway being sliced through the demo-
15 lition; buses grind below him, on the promenade. An air-force jet
flies in off the sea, its line of flight an upward curve that brings it
into sudden visibility over the jagged tops of the houses across
the terrace from the Kirks' tall, thin house. He turns the corner;
he walks up the hill. The long latticed metal of a construction
20 crane swings into his eyeline, dangling a concrete beam. Up the
hill he goes, past the remnants of the old order, the scraps of
traditional Watermouth falling beneath the claims of the modern
city. There are small shops – a newsagent with a window display
of *The Naked Ape*, a greengrocer with a few crates of vegetables
25 standing outside under a leaky canvas awning, a family butcher
with a notice saying 'We keep our meat on ice in hot weather'.
There are small back-to-back houses, whose doors open directly
onto the street; the bulldozers soon will reach them. Higher on
the hill grow the new concrete towers. Before he reaches them
30 Howard turns to the left, into a square of small houses, mostly
flats and private hotels. His old blue minivan stands in a line of
cars beside the kerb, under a sodium streetlamp. He unlocks the
driver's door; he gets in; he turns the ignition twice to fire the
engine. He drives the van back and forth, to clear the space. Then
35 he drives out of the square, down through the busy traffic of the
hill, and back into the terrace.

Malcolm Bradbury   *The History Man* 1975

1 Explain the meaning of the phrase 'dentistry of demolition' (lines 4–5).
   What does the phrase tell us about the kind of urban area being described?

2 What kind of people live in the terrace? Why does Malcolm Bradbury
   supply the reader with this information?

3 Explain the effect of the following verbs:
   'heehaws'   (line 14)
   'sliced'   (line 14)
   'grind'   (line 15)

4 Select five details from the description which seem to you to contribute
   to the effect which Bradbury is trying to achieve.

It might be helpful at this stage to summarize some of the points which should be emerging as you read these descriptions:

1 First, and perhaps most important, note how each description creates a very definite 'atmosphere' or 'mood'. These writers have not focussed on urban life in a general and haphazard way: these descriptions communicate a very definite impression of what life is like in the particular urban area described.

2 One way in which a writer does this is by selecting the details which he includes very carefully. Every aspect which T. S. Eliot describes contributes something to the mood of loneliness and squalor which haunts the poem.

3 These details are often concrete. In Malcolm Bradbury's description we are told what book the newsagent is displaying in his window, we learn that the awning over the greengrocer's leaks, and that the butcher wants his customers to know that he keeps his meat hygienically in hot weather. The effect of such detail is to convince us of the reality of his picture. We are made to feel that this town exists.

4 The way in which these writers draw upon the different senses also contributes to this feeling of reality. Visual details tend, naturally enough, to predominate. We can *see* 'the empty buses . . . rush past the open end of Terry Street', and the jets flying over 'the jagged tops' of Malcolm Bradbury's terrace. But the other senses are also utilized to help build up a complete description. There is the *sound* of the 'faint latest tunes' heard through the curtains in Terry Street, and in the Bradbury description there is the 'heehaw' of the police cars and the 'grinding' of the buses. In the poem by T. S. Eliot there is the *smell* of the steaks and the smoke. In Malcolm Bradbury's description we can feel the *touch* of the rain on Howard's hair while in Eliot's poem the leaves are 'wrapped' round our feet.

5 Finally, it is worth noting how the occasional image can arrest the reader's attention and communicate a sharp sense of what the writer wants to evoke. Think again how Malcolm Bradbury conjures up a picture of the half-destroyed terrace through the image of 'the curious dentistry of demolition'.

Your own writing

☐ Now write a description of one of the following subjects. Use between 350 and 500 words.

> ☐ Decide what impression of the place you want to create before you start to write.
>
> ☐ Build your description round carefully chosen details.
>
> ☐ Draw upon the different senses.
>
> ☐ Use images and comparisons where it might help to sharpen your description.

    a) Your school at night

    b) A crowded holiday resort

    c) A wood in mid-summer

    d) A ruined building

    e) A motorway service station

Describing personal experiences

So far in this chapter we have been concerned with descriptions of places. The examination boards often set descriptive essays of this kind, so it is important that you feel confident in tackling essays of the 'Your school at night' type. It is, however, worth remembering that two other types of essay, equally common in the examination, can also profit from effective passages of description. Firstly, there is the kind of essay question which asks you to write about something that you have done or which has happened to you; and, secondly, there is the question which involves you in telling a story. The two extracts which follow illustrate these two types of essay. Each gains much of its impact from the descriptive touches which the writer has included. Read each passage and answer the questions set on it.

In this first passage Al Alvarez describes a difficult rock climb up a sea cliff in Devon.

> Even to the most hardened eye it is an imposing place: a big, impending wall with the sea battering along its base out to a ragged headland, and the vast mouth of a cave opening on its right. There are climbs that thread improbably through the over-hangs on the cave's lip, with a hundred or more feet of space between the rock and the surging water; these look, quite simply, impossible. In comparison, the line of Moonraker is at least obvious: a series of cracks splitting the overhanging wall. It seems the most natural line on the cliff, but serious, straight up and down, not to be fooled with. Looked at from the opposite side of the cave, it seems to overhang from bottom to top. As it happens,

this is not a trick of perspective; the rock leans out on you continuously, right up to the last few feet. Mercifully, the holds are generous, but you need strong arms and steady nerves.

You need them, in fact, even before you get to the foot of the climb proper. The top of Berry Head is a flat, pleasant, blowy place where couples and children and dogs wander among the ruins of what was once a Napoleonic fort, the Old Redoubt. But the grass on the side of the bay opposite the cliff steepens rapidly, then becomes bare rock overhanging the sea; another world, not for tourists. You step blind round a corner of sheer rock and move carefully down into the vast, dank mouth of the cave. It seems as big as a cathedral: a black, thundering dome, like a lunatic's skull, water boiling along its floor, birds flitting in the dark air. Rock pigeons, guillemots and kittiwakes all nest there.

The chances are that your feet will be wet before you even reach the climb, since the long traverse round the cave is just above the water-line – if you are lucky and the sea is docile. But the traverse, which starts easily enough, becomes progressively harder, so you may have more than your feet wet by the time you reach the piton* stance a few feet above the water under the lowest of the inevitable overhangs. You dangle from the pegs, the sea banging and sucking at your feet. Above, what little you can see of the rock leans steadily out. The longer you hang there, the more deeply you ponder the climber's perennial question: how on earth did I allow myself to get into a situation like this?

Al Alvarez from *Hard Rock*   edited by Ken Wilson 1975

* piton: a small metal spike which climbers hammer into the rock in order to secure themselves to the cliff.

1 What impression of the cliff does Alvarez create in the first sentence? What words in this sentence are particularly important in creating this impression?

2 Why in the second paragraph does he describe the cliff top?

3 In this second paragraph, he compares the cave to two things. What are these things, and what does each comparison add to the picture which you have of the cave?

4 Do you feel that the description here makes it easier for you to understand what doing the climb was like? Or would you rather Alvarez had written immediately about what happened on the climb?

Description in narrative

In this second passage, which is from a novel called *The Bird of Night*, the descriptive details serve to create the tense and sinister atmosphere which hangs over the scene.

I see every detail of that house in my mind, the uneven arrangement of the bricks, and the way the window-ledges were
sunken in the middle, as though under the press of some
heavy weight.

The sun was shining still but it was bitterly cold, the wind
came howling down all the alleyways and I wore no overcoat.
I felt unreal walking through the streets, unable to believe
that I had come here. The house was in the lower part of the
town, in a mean, dank street, and I found it with some
difficulty. It was not what I knew of Oxford, yet Francis was
already known as a poet and he was not poor.

The curtains hung heavy at the windows, grass grew out of
cracks between the grey roof-slates. I rang the bell and
knocked. No one answered. I went in. Stairs led off to the
right but it was quite dark and I could not find any light
switch. The hallway smelled sour. If I close my eyes now, I
am standing there on the cracked black and white tiles of the
floor.

Then I went further, groping about from door to door, and up
two flights of stairs until I found him.

Both the curtains and the blinds of his sitting-room were
tightly drawn, no thread of daylight could get through them.
He was sitting in an armchair and there was an old-fashioned
lantern torch beside him. The bulb had almost gone out and
the light came and went, a dim blue-yellow. The fire was
banked high with coal and logs and smoking hard, a great
billow of it came out into the room as I opened the door.

'Francis . . .'

He scarcely glanced up. And then I felt uncertain, I felt
foolish, if he had asked me to explain why I had come I could
not have done so. But he said nothing and, after a moment, I
went into the room. I dreamed about it often later, saw the
faint glow from the fire, and his figure, hunched down in the
big chair and in the dream, I was always afraid.

'What's wrong?'

He looked up. He had taken off his spectacles and it was as
though I were seeing his face as it really was for the first time.

Susan Hill   *The Bird of Night* 1972

1 Why, in fact, does the narrator remember every detail of the house? What
   does the description of the window ledges immediately suggest about the
   house?

2 What impression of the house do you form from details given later in the
   passage of its outside appearance?

3 This description draws upon four of the five senses: sight, sound, smell,
   and touch. Give examples of each of these senses.

Your own writing

Not all essays about personal experiences and stories demand huge slabs of descriptive writing. Indeed, it is easy to overdo the effect, and you will have noted how Susan Hill built her effect up through odd details rather than through a lengthy paragraph of description.

☐ Bearing this warning in mind, choose one of the following topics and write an essay of 350–500 words upon it. Each topic is the kind of subject which could benefit from the intelligent use of description.

a) Children often have places of their own where they go to day-dream or play, perhaps an old attic or forgotten barn, a hidden cave or a hollow tree, a ruined house or a scrap yard, or even a ghostly, disused graveyard.

Write about the special places of your childhood. Try to express the atmosphere of the places and the feelings which they aroused in you.

b) Write on what *one* of the following suggests to you:

Either

> I have watched the street it stood in
> fall to the bulldozers, house by house
> each day a bit more sky:
> old man, the bulldozers have gone away
> and your house is still there
> its red front door still saying Number 14
> its windows hooded with corrugated iron
> jagged against the sky, its time come
> and gone, waiting for one more stroke.

Or

> We crossed by ferry to the bare island
> where sheep and cows stared coldly through the wind –
> the sea behind us with its silver water,
> the silent ferryman standing in the stern
> clutching his coat about him like old iron.

Or

> Walking in the scythed churchyard, around the locked church,
> Walking among the oaks and snails and mossed inscriptions
> At first we failed to find the grave.

c) Describe the scene outside a large sports stadium immediately before an important match.

d) Roads to Nowhere
Use the picture on page 40 as a starting-point for a piece of writing *relevant* to it or to this title.

e) Write whatever is suggested to you by ONE of the following extracts:

Either   An omnibus across the bridge
                Crawls like a yellow butterfly,
                And, here and there, a passer-by
                Shows like a little restless midge.
                Big barges full of yellow hay
                Are moved across the shadowy wharf,
                And, like a yellow silken scarf,
                The thick fog hangs along the quay.

Or   But when at dusk with steaming nostrils home
                They came, they seemed gigantic in the gloom,
                And warm and glowing with mysterious fire
                That lit their smouldering bodies in the mire.

Or   I hear the cries of evening, while the paw
                Of dark creeps up the turf:
                Sheep bleating, swaying gull's cry, the rook's caw,
                The hammering surf.

f) Write on any idea which the picture printed on page 41 suggests to you. (Any reasonably imaginative response is acceptable but some degree of relevance is expected.)

Chapter Two

Reading and writing about people

From primary school onwards you have probably written countless stories about different sorts of people: parents, teachers, policemen, and so on. If you choose to write a story in the examination, then the mark you gain will depend to a large extent on how successful you are in describing the people who figure in your story. What we are going to study in this unit is how you as a writer can bring the people you write about to life so that they are as vivid to your readers as they are to you.

Artists, like writers, often try to capture what is unique about somebody's personality.

☐ Study these portraits by three different artists. In each case write down all you can about the appearance, character and mood of the person portrayed.

Girl at the gate by Clausen

Study of Ossie Clark
by Hockney

Francis Bacon by Freud

Physical appearance

When we meet someone new, it is often what they look like which strikes us first. In each of the following extracts the writer concentrates on physical appearance. We are not told anything much about what any of these people is like as a person. Nor do we see any of them do anything or hear them say anything. We can, however, form an impression of their personalities from the details we are given of their physical appearance.

☐ Read the following extracts. After each extract write down:

the details which strike you as most vivid

the impression you have formed of the character's general personality.

When Goldfinger had stood up, the first thing that struck Bond was that everything was out of proportion. Goldfinger was short, not more than five feet tall, and on top of the thick body and blunt peasant legs, was set almost directly into the shoulders, a huge, and it seemed, exactly round head. It was as if Goldfinger had been put together with bits of other people's bodies. Nothing seemed to belong. Perhaps, Bond thought, it was to conceal his ugliness that Goldfinger made such a fetish of sunburn. Without the red brown camouflage the pale body would be grotesque. The face, under the cliff of crew-cut carroty hair, was startling, without being as ugly as the body. It was moon-shaped without being moon-like. The forehead was fine and high and the thin sandy brows were level above the large light blue eyes fringed with pale lashes. The nose was fleshily aquiline between high cheek bones and cheeks that were more muscular than fat. The mouth was thin and dead straight, but beautifully drawn. The chin and jaws were firm and glinted with health. To sum up, thought Bond, it was the face of a thinker, perhaps a scientist, who was ruthless, sensual, stoical and tough. An odd combination. . . .

Ian Fleming   *Goldfinger* 1959

A stoutly built fellow of about five and thirty, in a black velveteen coat, very soiled drab breeches, lace-up half boots, and grey cotton stockings, which enclosed a very bulky pair of legs, with large swelling calves – the kind of legs that, in such costume, always look in an unfinished and incomplete state without a set of fetters to garnish them. He had a brown hat on his head, and a dirty belcher handkerchief around his neck; with the long, frayed ends of which he smeared the beer from his face as he spoke; disclosing, when he had done so, a broad heavy countenance with a beard of three days' growth; and two scowling eyes; one of which displayed various parti-coloured symptoms of having been recently damaged by a blow.

Charles Dickens   *Oliver Twist* 1838

☐ Treat these photographs in the same way as the prose extracts. After you have studied each photograph write down:

the details which strike you as most vivid

the impression which you have formed of the character's personality.

Nyokabi called him. She was a small, black woman, with a bold but grave face. One could tell by her small eyes full of life and warmth that she had once been beautiful. But time and bad conditions do not favour beauty. All the same, Nyokabi had retained her full smile – a smile that lit up her dark face.

Ngugi Wa Thiong 'O   *Weep not, Child* 1964

He has red hair, very red, close curling, and a pale face, long in shape, with straight good features and little rather queer whiskers that are as red as his hair. His eyebrows are somehow darker; they look particularly arched and as if they might move a great deal. His eyes are sharp, strange – awfully; but I only know clearly that they are rather small and very fixed. His mouth's wide and his lips are thin, and except for his little whiskers he's quite clean shaven. He gives me a sort of sense of looking like an actor.

Henry James   *The Turn of the Screw* 1898

He was a small, wiry man. His hair had turned grey relatively early on and there was a smooth, glistening bald patch on the crown of his head. This combined with a sharp, prominent nose and a pair of penetrating, deepset eyes lent him an air of ferocious distinction. In later years he sprouted a moustache – looked after with fanatical care – which suited him. His lips were pinched and thin and his voice escaped through them like steam through the apertures of a whistling kettle. The analogy held in more ways than one. His voice was high and piping and querulous and the longer he talked (it made little difference whether the conversation excited him or not), the more high and piping and querulous did it become. He walked with a jaunty, hopping stride.

Shiva Naipaul   *The Chip-Chip Gatherers* 1961

Although you will no doubt have preferred some of these descriptions to others, they are all memorable in that the writers have built up their descriptions through the use of carefully chosen detail. The details which you include in your own descriptions are extremely important. Consider, for instance, how much each of these sentences says about the person described.

Father Thomas's long narrow nose was oddly twisted at the end; it gave him the effect of smelling sideways at some elusive odour.
Graham Greene   *A Burnt-Out Case* 1961

Her face was old now, a used crumpled envelope, but a child still looked out from her eyes.
Nina Bawden   *George Beneath a Paper Moon* 1974

☐ Now write two descriptions of people you know in which you concentrate on their physical appearance. Use no more than 150 words for each description.

Significant actions

When we come to know someone better, we start noticing how they act. This might be a matter of some small but characteristic gesture, like, perhaps, the way Father Thomas seems to smell sideways 'at some elusive odour', or of some more general action that says something highly significant about the person in question.

The next two extracts illustrate how vividly alive a character can become if the writer concentrates on a particular gesture.

When Bretherton woke, beer-flushed, with belches of discomfort, at the sound of the caddy spoon on the side of the teapot, he looked like one of those model porkers, fat and pinkish, squatting on its hind-legs with an advertisement for sausages in its lap, that you see in butchers' windows. The sausages were his fingers. They glistened, a pink-grey colour, as they grasped tremulously at each other and then at his tobacco-yellow moustache.

H. E. Bates   *Love for Lydia* 1952

– and from time to time, as he looked down at his green soup, he also looked slightly askance at Rose Vassiliou's hand, which was crumbling to pieces, with an untiring restless purposeless motion, the brown wholemeal bread on her plate. It interested him, this hand, and he remembered the touch of it in greeting: it had been light and dry, and the back of it was brown and slightly crazed like an old earthenware pot. He could not recollect that he had ever seen so fine a mesh of wrinkles, that had about them no suggestion of age, or of loosening of the skin: they were of the surface, like small scratches. The hand looked not old, but child-like. One nail only had been bitten: a confined neurosis, attached to the index finger. There was a ring on the middle finger with a white stone in it: a sardonyx. The hand hovered over the bread, restlessly plucking and seizing and crumbling, like a friend or a small bird.

Margaret Drabble   *The Needle's Eye* 1972

☐ Re-read each passage. What is the action in each passage which sums up the character?

47

☐ Each of these photographs shows someone gesturing with their hands. Try and explain exactly how each person is using their hands. Are they explaining, describing, commanding, enquiring or something else?

Is it possible to describe these actions in words, or can the photographer (or artist) capture a person's actions in a way that a writer cannot?

These next three extracts focus on their subjects in a rather more general way. The writer's technique is still, however, to focus on an action or way of behaving which is characteristic or significant of the character described.

He had a shameless pride in his physical strength; a pride reinforced by the smallness of his build. "Don't let my shortness fool you," he was in the habit of saying. "Some of the greatest men in the world was short." He was addicted to showing off his muscles in public. On the slightest pretext he would roll up his shirtsleeves and flex his biceps for the benefit of some startled visitor to the house, challenging him to do better. Few of them ever could. The satisfaction these displays afforded him never diminished. And, after the display, there was the homily. "The most important duty a man have in this world is to keep himself strong and healthy and in trim. How you think I manage to get where I is today?"

His day began and ended with exercises. He kept in his bedroom an impressive array of muscle-building apparatus which he allowed no one to touch but himself. In his passion for exercising was revealed another of his quirks of character. Despite his much vaunted enthusiasm for the wellbeing of the body, he never actively encouraged other people to follow his example. The well-being of the body which he lauded was the well-being of his own body. While eager to demonstrate the results of his exertions, the exertions themselves he surrounded in secrecy. He considered it an invasion of privacy to set eyes on him during the periods he set aside for his exercise and it was a prohibition strictly enforced. When he was asked – much of the time out of politeness, but he did not recognize this – about the techniques he employed, he betrayed a reticence the true import of which none could fail to understand: his preoccupation with health, universal as it pretended to be, began and ended with himself. Not only was he not interested in the health of his fellows: he was positively displeased if they decided to tread too zealously in his footsteps.

Shiva Naipaul   *The Chip-Chip Gatherers*   1961

1 Summarize in one sentence what we learn about this man in these two paragraphs.
2 Why do you think that the man is secretive about the 'techniques' he employed'?
3 What impression of his personality do you have from what you are told here?

Boy driving his father to confession

Four times now I have seen you as another
Man, a grown-up friend, less than a father;
Four times found chinks in the paternal mail
To find you lost like me, quite vulnerable.
There was the time when my child brother died
And in the porch, among the men, you cried.
Again, last year, I was shocked at your tears
When my mother's plane took off. In twelve years
You had not been apart for one whole day
Till this long-talked-of, two-week holiday:
I left you lonely at the barrier,
Was embarrassed later when you stood a beer.
The third time you made a man of me
By telling me an almost smutty story
In a restaurant toilet. We both knew
This was an unprecedented breakthrough.

To-day, a sinner, and shy about it,
You asked me to drive up to church, and sit
Morose as ever, telling me to slow
On corners or for potholes that I know
As well as you do. What is going on
Under that thick grey skull? What confession
Are you preparing. Do you tell sins as I would?
Does the same hectic rage in our one blood?
Here at the churchyard I am slowing down
To meet you, the fourth time, on common ground.
You grunt, and slam the door. I watch another
Who gropes as awkwardly to know his father.

Seamus Heaney 1970

1 What four incidents explain the poet's feeling about his father?

2 In no more than 50 of your own words describe what this feeling is.

Now she sat there, tired and comfortable, in a deep arm chair,
with her feet curled up under her, looking at the pictures. She
wore a long wool skirt, and expensive shoes. She was tall, slight
and bony, her face was lined and hard and sweet. She had the
gallant air of a woman fighting a losing battle, but nobody could
guess the terms of her defeat, for she was discreet and silent
about herself. She had a well-shaped mouth, curiously curved,
with thin and conscious delicate lips, a careful and precise and
gentle way of speech. Her hair was dyed. It had turned, in the
course of nature, from brown to a miserable, mustardy yellowy
fuzzy grey, and so she dyed it, back to its original brown. It was
her one weak gesture, and it was a realistic one, for she did, as she

50

had said to Frances one day some years ago, look like the Witch of Endor with it undyed. And who wants to look like *that*? she had said. It isn't fair to other people, she had said. Who could tell what vanity lay concealed in her? Certainly she always wore extremely expensive shoes. Now they were tucked under her, out of sight. . . .

Margaret Drabble   *The Realms of Gold* 1975

1 This paragraph tells us a great deal about the woman's physical appearance, but the author places special emphasis on the fact that she has dyed her hair. What does this fact lead you to feel about the woman?

2 In no more than 50 of your own words describe this woman's personality.

Conversations

If describing someone's behaviour is one way in which we can communicate to the reader something of what they are like, then having them speak is another equally revealing technique. You only have to listen to any of your friends to know that how they talk and what they talk about can be immensely revealing.

In the passage which follows, the writer, Alan Garner, says nothing directly about what his characters are like. There is no physical description of them, and very little significant action. If, however, we read the conversation carefully, we can learn a good deal about both Tom and his parents.

'Any mail?'[1]

'Aunty Evelyn and Uncle Peter, Aunty Marina, Mr and Mrs Harrison: one from London. Father'll be home shortly. And I don't want you in the kitchen. It'll spoil the treat.'

'I'll revise my Greek,' said Tom. He lay on his bed and put the cans over his ears.

The caravan dipped as Tom's father came up the steps from the carport. He was holding a square box against his chest. Tom felt his parents move about the kitchen. He gave them five
10 minutes, then closed his book.

'Ready?' he said.

'Yes.'

He went into the kitchen. They were sitting at the table.

'"– Happy Birthday, dear To-hom;

'"Happy Birthday to you!"'

He looked at the cake in the middle of the table. 'Did you make that?'

'Is it all right?' said his father.

'It's incredible.'

[1] The conversation in the extract is punctuated by single quote marks, not double as on page 49. We have followed the style of the original published text. See page 173.

20   The cake was the shape of a railway engine, the icing meticu-
lous and coloured, with his father's regimental crest on the side.
        'Do you like it?'
        'It's –'
        'I was plundering my mind for a theme,' said his father, 'a
motif: I thought we needed to show –'
        'It's –'
        '– We needed to show you were going far.'
        'It's great.'
        'He thinks a lot of you,' said Tom's mother. 'You don't like it,
30   do you?'
        'It must have taken ages –'
        'Oh, an hour here and there –'
        'He was up all times last week. Didn't come home till three
this morning.'
        'Thanks,' said Tom. 'Thanks very much. Thanks.'
        'Presents next,' said his mother.
        'We didn't know what to give you –'
        'They're only odds and ends –'
        'You shouldn't have bothered –'
40   'And you're growing so fast –'
        'Am I?'
        'We couldn't think –'
        'Anyway – '
        'It's all right,' said Tom.
        'Well, open them.'
        The first packet was a tie and two pairs of socks.
        'You can change them if they're no use.'
        'No. They're great. Thanks.'
        'Or I'll have 'em,' said his father.
50   'You won't!' said Tom. He unfastened his mother's present. It
was a notebook with a padded binding, and the title in gold leaf:
'Books I Have Read'.
        'It's got columns for Dates, Names and Comments', said his
mother.
        'Yes. Yes. Smashing. Thanks.'
        'That's all,' said his father. 'We didn't know what would do
for, for, well, what you might call a real present.'
        'Don't worry,' said Tom.
        'But we're getting one: later, like.'
60   'Actually,' said Tom, 'the money would do.'
        'It would not!' said his mother. 'You'd only spend it.'
        'It's like gift tokens,' said his father. 'There's no thought
behind them.'
        'We're saving up,' said his mother. 'You'll have a special one
for Christmas.'
        'Now then.' His father cleared the wrapping paper away. He
folded each piece, and arranged the presents either side of the
cake, propping the book against a plate. Buns, trifle, jam tarts and

52

two different flavours of jelly: and lemonade. 'Now then.' He
70 checked the camera. 'Pretend to cut the cake. Ready? Hold it.'
Flash.
'One more.'
Tom sat and looked at the table. 'I'm very grateful –'
'Of course, love,' said his mother. 'Now have some trifle. It's
your favourite.'
'What's Janet sent?' said his father.
'A card.'
'No present?' said his mother.
'We'd arranged –'
80 'Nursing's not well salaried,' said his father. 'It's more what
you might call a vocation.'
'She'll have means.'
'She's living off her pay,' said Tom.
'Still, she might've sent something,' said his mother. 'She
could afford to go wherever it was she went this year.'
'Parcel post's often delayed –'.
'Give over,' said Tom's mother. 'Can't you see you're up-
setting him?'

Alan Garner   *Red Shift* 1973

1 In lines 22–8 his father keeps interrupting Tom. What does this suggest
about what each of them is feeling?

2 The following sentences are all spoken by Tom's mother:

'He thinks a lot of you. . . . You don't like it' (29–30)
'He was up all times last week. Didn't come home till three this morning.'
(33–4)
'It would not . . . You'd only spend it.' (61)
'Of course, love . . . Now have some trifle. It's your favourite.' (74–5)
'No present?' (78)
'Give over. . . . Can't you see you're upsetting him?' (87–8)

What impression do you form of her?

3 What can you deduce about Tom's personality from the way in which he
replies to his parents?

In this extract which you have just read, every line of dialogue has been
carefully chosen to reveal something about the character concerned. It is
also convincingly realistic. The interruptions, the embarrassments, the
quick ebb and flow of the speech all persuade the reader that the conversation could have happened. It is not, of course, easy to achieve these
effects but your own stories will become much more interesting and alive if
you can include passages of dialogue which seem similarly realistic.

Your own writing

☐ Choose *one* of the following incidents. Think hard about the personalities of the people involved, what they are like and how they might interact. In as realistic a fashion as you can, write the conversation which they might have.

a) A 12-year-old boy has been caught shoplifting. His mother has collected him from the police station and they are walking home.

b) A young teacher has come to school in jeans. The Headmaster disapproves and is talking to him in his study.

c) A man arrives home two hours late from work. He did not telephone and his dinner is ruined. His wife meets him at the door.

☐ Write a conversation for one of these pairs of people.

Analysis of emotion and thought

The passages quoted so far in the chapter have one thing in common: you have had to reach your own conclusions about the character described from the evidence which the writer has given to you. The first group of passages concentrated on physical appearance, the second on behaviour, and the third extract from *Red Shift* showed how people can reveal a lot about themselves when they speak. There is, though, another strategy which a writer can adopt. He can tell you *directly* what a character is thinking and feeling. In real life, of course, this is something we can never be certain about, and one of the pleasures of reading novels is being able to see inside a character's mind and heart.

The passage which follows is from the Russian novel *Dr Zhivago*. Yury Zhivago has been having an affair with a woman called Lara. He still, however, loves his wife Tonya.

Yury was riding home from Yuryatin. He had made this journey countless times. He was so used to the road, that he was no longer aware of it, he hardly saw it.

Soon he would come to the crossroads in the forest where the way straight on led to Varykino and a path turned off to a fishing village on the river Sakma; here stood yet another hoarding advertising agricultural machinery; as usual, he would reach the crossroads at dusk.

10 It was now more than two months since that day when he went to town as usual but, instead of returning home the same afternoon, spent the night at Lara's and later told his family that he had been kept on business and had stayed at Samdevyatov's inn. He had long been calling Lara by her Christian name and saying 'thou' to her, though she still called him Zhivago. Yury was deceiving Tonya and what he concealed from her was becoming increasingly grave and illicit. This was something unheard of between them.

He worshipped Tonya. Her peace of mind meant more to him than anything in the world. He was ready to defend her honour

20 and was more sensitive to anything touching it than her father or herself. In defence of her pride he would have torn anyone apart with his own hands. And yet now he was offending against it himself.

At home he felt like a criminal. His family's ignorance of the truth, their unchanged affection, were a mortal torment to him. In the middle of a conversation he would suddenly be numbed by the recollection of his guilt and cease hearing a word of what was being said.

If this happened during a meal, his food stuck in his throat

30 and he put down his spoon and pushed away his plate. 'What is wrong with you?' Tonya would ask, puzzled. 'You must have had some bad news when you were in town. Has anyone been

arrested? Or shot? Tell me. Don't be frightened of upsetting me. You'll feel better when you've told me.'

Had he been unfaithful to her because he preferred another woman? No, he had made no comparison, no choice. He did not believe in 'free love' or in the 'right' to be carried away by his senses. To think or speak in such terms seemed to him degrading. He had never 'sown wild oats,' nor did he regard him-
40   self as a superhuman with special rights and privileges. Now he was crushed by the weight of his guilty conscience.

'What next?' he sometimes asked himself, and hoped wretchedly for some impossible, unexpected circumstance to solve his problem for him.

Boris Pasternak   *Dr Zhivago* 1958 (Russian edition)

1 In your own words, explain what Yury Zhivago's feelings are for Tonya.

2 What effect does his affair have on Yury Zhivago?

3 What do lines 35–40 tell us about the kind of man Yury is?

You should now have developed some understanding of the main ways in which it is possible for a writer to bring his characters to life. The four techniques which we have examined are:

- ☐ the description of physical appearance
- ☐ the description of typical or significant actions
- ☐ the writing of dialogue
- ☐ the direct analysis of emotion or thought

In practice, most writers tend, of course, to use all these different techniques when they write a story. They will switch quickly from one technique to another, and in your own writing you will probably find this the most helpful way to proceed. This is what happens in the last two examples.

☐ Read these passages and answer the questions which are set on them.

Pitchforked awake by a sharp pain in her back, Norah sat up in bed quickly, pushing at the mattress with her hands, making Mr Gawber's whole body leap. She switched on the bright bedside lamp, blinding her feebly inquiring husband, who turned and groaned. He lifted his pocket watch from the side table and swung it to his eye. It was just past eleven-thirty – he'd had one hour's sleep. Norah, motioning to stifle a sigh, managed to amplify it. She jerked on the bed, testing her back, drummed her legs and sighed again, drawing the noise slowly through a grievous scale, high to low, the sound of a person spinning down a deep shaft and never striking bottom, only whimpering at the end and growling into silence. They were both fully awake now, and in pyjamas and night-dress, their hair fluffed into tangled white wigs, they looked blanched and ancient, whitened by frailty, two-hundred years old. Mr Gawber quaked. The light jarred him like noise. Norah said, 'I can't sleep.'

Mr Gawber pretended not to hear; but how typical of her to wake him to tell him that! She was no solitary sufferer. She demanded a witness, involving him in her discomfort, made him endure it. Invariably she touched him with her pain, and there was not an upset she'd had that he had not somehow shared. She sighed, he groaned. It was in part the penalty of the double bed, marriage's narrow raft.

'Wake up, Rafie, I can't sleep.'

'What is it?' He exaggerated his drowsiness.

'I feel ghastly. Yes, I think I'm coming down with something.' She tried her fingers, tasted her tongue, blinked – to locate symptoms.

'Probably' – he yawned: a stage-yawn, almost a pronouncement – 'probably just wind.'

'No,' she insisted. 'I've pins and needles. A splitting headache. I've gone all hot.' She got a grip on her head and out of the corner of his eye Mr Gawber saw her swivel it. She looked as if she might be trying to unscrew it.

'Leave your head alone. You'll just make it worse.'

'I'm feverish.'

'Poor thing.' Without wishing to he yawned again, an authentic rebuke.

'You don't care.' She started to cry softly. 'Oh, my head. It won't stop.'

He said, 'I believe you're coming down with something.'

'It's flu,' she said and was calm. She listed her symptoms once more.

'I'm not surprised. There's a lot of it around. Thornquist was out all last week.'

He wanted to be sympathetic, but Norah's illnesses were always so laborious that it annoyed him to hear her complain of their annoyance. He resisted consoling her. Then her aches and pains gave him some satisfaction – she deserved them for the pain she caused him. By a queer process of reversal, charity made antagonistic, he came to enjoy hearing her say how it hurt.

The bright lamp knocked against his eyes. He said, 'Do turn the light off.'

'How can I find my medicine in the dark?'

She thumped the mattress again, bouncing him, and went to the bathroom, switching on lights. She returned with a bottle of Doctor Collis Browne's Mixture. It was an old bottle, containing a fluid now unlawfully potent, the active ingredient being opium. She was a regular user of patent medicines and pills: green lung tonic, fruit drops, stinging ointments, syrup of figs, dragees that stained her tongue purple. She was troubled by wind; she took iron for her blood. Old ailments, old cures. She measured the Collis Browne into a soup spoon and sucked it noisily.

'Do you a world of good,' Mr Gawber muttered.

Norah lay panting. Mr Gawber reached across and turned the light off. She snored.

Paul Theroux   *The Family Arsenal* 1976

1 What impression do you form of the character of

    a) Norah

    b) Mr Gawber?

2 How does Paul Theroux communicate to us what these people are like? Find one example of each of the four techniques of characterization which you have studied in the unit.

3 Which of these techniques do you feel is most important to the success of the characterization?

4 Do you find it possible to believe in these people? Or do you find the portraits too exaggerated? Give reasons for your answer.

Ursula went forward to the teachers' room that burrowed in a gloomy hole. She knocked timidly.

"Come in!" called a surprised man's voice, as from a prison cell. She entered the dark little room that never got any sun. The gas was lighted naked and raw. At the table a thin man in shirt-sleeves was rubbing a paper on a jelly-tray. He looked up at Ursula with his narrow, sharp face, said "Good morning," then turned away again, and stripped the paper off the tray, glancing at the violet-coloured writing transferred, before he dropped the curled sheet aside among a heap.

Ursula watched him fascinated. In the gaslight and gloom and the narrowness of the room, all seemed unreal.

"Isn't it a nasty morning," she said.

"Yes," he said, "it's not much of weather."

But in here it seemed that neither morning nor weather really existed. This place was timeless. He spoke in an occupied voice, like an echo. Ursula did not know what to say. She took off her waterproof.

"Am I early?" she asked.

The man looked first at a little clock, then at her. His eyes seemed to be sharpened to needle-points of vision.

"Twenty-five past," he said. "You're the second to come. I'm first this morning."

Ursula sat down gingerly on the edge of a chair, and watched his thin red hands rubbing away on the white surface of the paper, then pausing, pulling up a corner of the sheet, peering, and rubbing away again. There was a great heap of curled white-and-scribbled sheets on the table.

"Must you do so many?" asked Ursula.

Again the man glanced up sharply. He was about thirty or thirty-three years old, thin, greenish, with a long nose and a sharp face. His eyes were blue, and sharp as points of steel, rather beautiful, the girl thought.

"Sixty-three," he answered.

"So many!" she said, gently. Then she remembered.

"But they're not all for your class, are they?" she added.

"Why aren't they?" he replied, a fierceness in his voice.

Ursula was rather frightened by his mechanical ignoring of her, and his directness of statement. It was something new to her. She had never been treated like this before, as if she did not count, as if she were addressing a machine.

"It is too many," she said sympathetically.

"You'll get about the same," he said.

That was all she received. She sat rather blank, not knowing how to feel. Still she liked him. He seemed so cross. There was a queer, sharp, keen-edge feeling about him that attracted her and frightened her at the same time. It was so cold, and against his nature.

The door opened, and a short, neutral-tinted young woman of about twenty-eight appeared.

"Oh, Ursula!" the newcomer exclaimed. "You *are* here early! My word, I'll warrant you don't keep it up. That's Mr. Williamson's peg. *This* is yours. Standard Five teacher always has this. Aren't you going to take your hat off?"

Miss Violet Harby removed Ursula's waterproof from the peg on which it was hung, to one a little further down the row. She had already snatched the pins from her own stuff hat, and jammed them through her coat. She turned to Ursula, as she pushed up her frizzed, flat, dun-coloured hair.

"Isn't it a beastly morning," she exclaimed, "beastly! And if there's one thing I hate above another it's a wet Monday morning; – pack of kids trailing in anyhow-nohow, and no holding 'em –"

She had taken a black pinafore from a newspaper package, and was tying it round her waist.

"You've brought an apron, haven't you?" she said jerkily, glancing at Ursula. "Oh – you'll want one. You've no idea what a sight you'll look before half-past four, what with chalk and ink and kids' dirty feet. – Well, I can send a boy down to mamma's for one."

"Oh, it doesn't matter," said Ursula.

"Oh, yes – I can send easily," cried Miss Harby.

Ursula's heart sank. Everybody seemed so cocksure and so bossy. How was she going to get on with such jolty, jerky, bossy people? And Miss Harby had not spoken a word to the man at the table. She simply ignored him. Ursula felt the callous crude rudeness between the two teachers.

The two girls went out into the passage. A few children were already clattering in the porch.

"Jim Richards," called Miss Harby, hard and authoritative. A boy came sheepishly forward.

"Shall you go down to our house for me, eh?" said Miss Harby, in a commanding, condescending, coaxing voice. She did not wait for an answer. "Go down and ask mamma to send me one of my school pinas, for Miss Brangwen – shall you?"

The boy muttered a sheepish "Yes, Miss," and was moving away.

"Hey," called Miss Harby. "Come here – now what are you going for? What shall you say to mamma?"

"A school pina – " muttered the boy.

"'Please, Mrs. Harby, Miss Harby says will you send her another school pinafore for Miss Brangwen, because she's come without one.'"

"Yes, Miss," muttered the boy, head ducked, and was moving off. Miss Harby caught him back, holding him by the shoulder.

"What are you going to say?"

"Please, Mrs. Harby, Miss Harby wants a pinny for Miss Brangwin," muttered the boy very sheepishly.

"Miss *Brangwen*!" laughed Miss Harby, pushing him away. "Here, you'd better have my umbrella – wait a minute."

The unwilling boy was rigged up with Miss Harby's umbrella, and set off.

"Don't take long over it," called Miss Harby, after him. Then she turned to Ursula, and said brightly:

"Oh, he's a caution, that lad – but not bad, you know."

"No," Ursula agreed, weakly.

D. H. Lawrence   *The Rainbow* 1915

1 What techniques does Lawrence use to describe the man who is sitting at the table?

2 How does this man behave towards Ursula?

3 What sort of person does he seem to be?

4 In what sort of manner does Miss Harby talk to Ursula and Jim Richards? Does she in fact treat them any differently?

5 What is your impression of Miss Harby?

6 Ursula is clearly the central character here, and we see things through her eyes. At several points in the story Lawrence tells us what she is feeling. In your own words sum up

    a) her general emotional state

    b) her reaction to the man

    c) her reaction to Miss Harby

Your own writing

In order to create vivid and realistic characters who will interest anyone who reads your work you need to know something of the different techniques writers use to describe people. In the earlier part of this chapter you studied these techniques, and you should now have a firm grasp of what each has to offer. Before starting to write anything, however, it is vital to have thought long and hard about the person whom you want to describe. You need to know as much as you can about him or her, more than you know about most people in real life, if this character is to come alive for your readers.

☐ Suppose, for instance, that you want to write about a teacher you had in primary school. Before starting to write, jot down and answer questions like these:

> What did she look like?
> How old was she?
> What did she wear?
> How did she behave? (Can you think of any one incident that is typical of her?)
> What sort of things was she interested in?
> How did she treat the children?

As this is a real person then your memory will be important, though you will no doubt have to make up answers to some of the questions which seem significant to you. If the person is someone imaginary, then you will have to make up all the answers. *In either case the important thing is to know as much as you can about the person before you start to write the actual description.*

☐ Now answer one of the following questions. Each question has been taken from an examination paper, and each demands that you develop a convincing portrait of one or more people.

a) You are a voluntary worker helping needy people in your district. Describe what you do, what happens to you, whom you meet, and what your feelings are about your work.

b) *Either:* Shop assistants – by a customer. *Or:* Customers – by a shop assistant.

c) Describe a person towards whom your feelings have changed in some way since your first meeting, explaining why this has happened.

d) Use the picture printed on the facing page as a basis for your writing.

e) Choose one of the passages on the facing page and write about what the passage suggests to you. You may include the passage chosen as part of a story.

She walked slowly back in the direction of the pier for want of something better to do and paid the ten pence that allowed her to walk its long length. Couples passed her, arm in arm or hand in hand, heads together, whispering their secrets. Everyone had someone to care for and to care for them. Except her.

I swallowed heavily and pressed the door bell. I realized the majority of people were already there. I caught glimpses of unknown faces drifting across the window and heard excited voices. I wished I hadn't come.

Chapter Three

Reading and writing stories

In this chapter you will read and study a number of stories and extracts from stories. Each of the passages quoted will demonstrate a particular aspect of the novelist's or short story writer's craft. The questions set on the passages are intended to direct your attention to what is particularly significant in each passage. When you have read these passages and answered the questions set on them, you should have a much more detailed understanding of how a good story is constructed. This understanding should, in turn, help you to write more powerful and effective stories of your own.

It is hard to imagine a story which is not in some way or another about people, and most writers make considerable use of descriptive passages or touches. You should, therefore, refer to Chapters One and Two for advice about these aspects of writing a story.

Keeping the story simple

If you were to write a novel, you would have two hundred or more pages in which to develop your story. It is more likely, however, that you will be writing short stories of, at the most, a few pages. In the examination you will have to concentrate everything you want to say into about 500 words. It is not, therefore, very wise to attempt to write a story which involves a large number of people or which has a very complicated plot. The best short stories are, in fact, often the simplest.

The two stories which follow are both simple in that the writer has chosen to focus on just one event. Read each story and answer the questions set on it.

Crossroads Nowhere

I turned my back on the whirlpool of Marble Arch, the currents of cars that careered in and out of the Park, the crowd that shuffled and elbowed its way down Oxford Street, and began to walk up the Edgware Road. The evening had turned sharp, and the wind cut waist-high along the buildings. I turned up the collar of my coat, and stuffed my hands into the caves of my pockets. It was past supper-time, but the rooms where the young men and women sat perched on stools looked long and forbidding, the fragrance of fried chips and the towers of porkpies blunted the edge of my appetite. The vortex of Marble Arch drew a mixed crowd, but the permanent signs – the firmly shuttered cigarette kiosk and the pile of unsold *Evening Standards* – were desperately English. The tall Indian and the two girls speaking German who clutched his arm, the sprinkling of foreigners that salted and seasoned the pavement-crowds appeared as if drawn from the cones and threads of small streets that issue into the highway, as if thrust up from some vast, submerged international underworld that crouched behind the brassy frontage of the Odeon. In the surging throng I hardly remarked the coated form that passed me as I walked, and the voice that said, "A'right, sagga boy" was lost almost at once in the incessant hum of traffic. I stopped.

The lilt was unmistakable: West Indian – a greeting offered and over, like the flash of a trafficator or the sudden glare of a headlamp – a single sounded note of recognition that required no acknowledgement. For the form had passed on, that curious West Indian roll carrying him around the corner and up towards the Corner House. I turned, and walked quickly after him.

"Hey, boy," I said, "you know a good place to eat?" He was tall, the face behind the thin edge of stubble that followed the line of his chin burnt bronze beneath the neon. He wore a coat, but no tie, and his shirt was collarless and open at the throat with a kind of summer abandon.

I had surprised him. "Anywhere good round here to eat?" He smiled at this and relaxed. "Well, lemme see now . . ." He began to wave his hand, leisurely withdrawn from his pocket, in an expansive arc that gestured me towards the farther limits of Oxford Street, and seemed to embrace the whole of north London. "If you walk as far as de traffic-lite – not dese here, you know, two or t'ree after . . ." I looked in the direction but the traffic lights winked exasperatingly at me from every intersection . . . "an' turn lef', and lef' at the nex' street, you come to a arcade on the rite han' side: tack thru' there, swing roun' an' ease down the road a piece, an' is there, yu' boun' to see it." His eyes searched my uncomprehending face, and he permitted himself the luxury of an explanation.

"Tha's the Wes' Indian place you ask me for."

I grinned. "You work roun' here?"

"A doin' a job at Lyons, na? Til' a get a real work." He was preparing to go.

I tried to think of something I could say to keep him. "You like London?"

He smiled. "A livin'. After you dead a'ready. Whe' you goin' do, boy?"

"I'm Jamaican too," I said. "Where you from, Kingston?"

He nodded. "Tha's a far place, boy." He looked down the long stretch of Bayswater Road as if he expected to catch a glimpse of the Atlantic.

What could I say? That I hadn't heard words slip off the tongue like that, like a cascade of minted pennies, for months, that we should go somewhere and talk, that we had something to say? Out of a thousand mocking murmurs in a thousand foreign tongues, his had caught my ear, as the single call of a fisherman across the harbour brings the pasteboard canoes dancing and jigging together from the darkness. The when and the why of him, and that we were *not* strangers, might have filled a thousand fictions: exile gave a strange singularity to our meeting. The wind caught at these half-formed questions, and the shrug of his narrow shoulders helped me to silence. In spite of the huge trucks that burrow through Hammersmith to the Great West Road, or the vans that funnel their way to the river, in spite of the myriad taxis that weave and wind through the backstreets and knit the city together as with a network of veins – in spite of its restless, ceaseless activity, London is full of surprising silences. Livin'. After you dead a'ready. Whe' you goin' do, boy? For a moment our eyes crossed, the look framing his story better than his lips, the eyes dark without self-pity, the mouth smiling, unresigned: then the lights changed on us, orange, green and the traffic was gone.

"Right." I nodded. He nodded. Finished. Ships that pass. London opened its dark jaws, yawned once, and swallowed him like a snake.

Stuart Hall 1960

1 What exactly does happen in this story?
2 The story begins with a description of the Marble Arch area of London. What sort of place does this seem to be?
3 What is London compared to in the last sentence of the story?
4 What does this image tell you about how the narrator feels at this point?
5 Why does the narrator chase after the West Indian man who has spoken to him?
6 Why in the last paragraph does he compare the man's speech to the 'single call of a fisherman'?
7 Although little actually happens in the story, the reader is left with a strong sense of what it is like to be a stranger in a big city. It is this experience of being a stranger which is really the point or subject of the story. In your own words describe what this experience is like.

Although there is considerably more action in the next story, it is again just one event which is being described.

One of them shouted a warning, but it was too late. The leaves brushed him down almost delicately. The small branches en-caged him. And then the tree and the whole hill crushed him together.

A man breathlessly said that a woodman was trapped beneath a tree. The doctor asked the dispenser to find out exactly where: then suddenly picked up his own phone, interrupted her and spoke himself. He must know exactly where. Which was the nearest gate in the nearest field? Whose field? He would need a stretcher. His own stretcher had been left in hospital the day before. He told the dispenser to phone immediately for an ambulance and tell it to wait by the bridge which was the nearest point on the road. At home in the garage there was an old door off its hinges. Blood plasma from the dispensary, door from the garage. As he drove through the lanes he kept his thumb on the horn the whole time, partly to warn oncoming traffic, partly so that the man under the tree might hear it and know that the doctor was coming.

After five minutes he turned off the road and drove uphill, into the mist. As often up there above the river, it was a very white mist, a mist that seemed to deny all weight and solidity. He had to stop twice to open gates. The third gate was already slightly open, so he drove through it without stopping. It swung back and crashed against the rear of the Land Rover. Some sheep, startled, appeared and disappeared into the mist. All the while he had his thumb on the horn for the woodman to hear. After one more field he saw a figure waving behind the mist – as if he were trying to wipe clean a vast steamed-up window.

When the doctor reached him the man said: "He's been screaming ever since. He's suffering something terrible doctor." The man would tell the story many times, and the first would be tonight in the village. But it was not yet a story. The advent of the doctor brought the conclusion much nearer, but the accident was not yet over: the wounded man was still screaming at the other two men who were hammering in wedges preparatory to lifting the tree.

"Christ let me alone." As he cried 'alone' the doctor was beside him. The wounded man recognized the doctor; his eyes focused. For him too the conclusion was nearer and this gave him the courage to be quieter. Suddenly it was silent. The men had stopped hammering but were still kneeling on the ground. They knelt and looked at the doctor. His hands are at home on a body. Even these new wounds which had not existed twenty minutes before were familiar to him. Within seconds of being beside the man he injected morphine. The three onlookers were relieved by the doctor's presence. But now his very sureness made it seem to them that he was part of the accident: almost its accomplice.

"He had a chance," said one of the kneeling men, "when Harry here shouted but he went and turned about the wrong way."

The doctor set up the plasma for a transfusion into the arm. As he moved around, he explained what he was doing to try to reassure the others.

"I shouted at him," said Harry, "he could have got clear if he'd looked sharp."

"He would have got clear like that," said the third.

As the morphine worked, the wounded man's face relaxed and his eyes closed. It was then as though the relief he felt was so intense that it reached the others.

"He's lucky to be alive," said Harry.

"He could have got clear like that," said the third.

The doctor asked them if they could shift the tree.

"I reckon we can if we are three now."

Nobody was kneeling any longer. The three woodsmen were standing, impatient to begin. The mist was getting whiter. The moisture was condensing on the half-empty bottle of plasma. The doctor noticed that this fractionally changed its colour, making it look yellower than normal.

"I want you to lift," he said, "while I put a splint on his leg."

When the wounded man felt the reverberations in the tree as they levered it, he began to moan again.

"We could injure him worse than ever," said Harry, "getting him out." He could see the crushed leg underneath like a dog killed on the road.

"Just hold it steady," said the doctor.

Again the doctor, whom they knew so well, seemed the accomplice of disaster as he worked under the tree on the leg the fourth of them would lose.

"We'd never believed you'd got here so quick, doc," said the third.

"You know Sleepy Joe?" asked the doctor. "He was trapped under a tree for twelve hours before any help came."

He gave instructions on how to lift the wounded man on to the door and then into the back of the Land Rover.

"You'll be all right now Jack," said one of them to the wounded man whose face was as damp and pallid as the mist. The third touched his shoulder.

The ambulance was waiting at the bridge. When it had driven off, Harry turned to the doctor confidentially.

"He's lost his leg," he said, "hasn't he?"

"No, he won't lose his leg," said the doctor.

The woodman walked slowly back up to the forest. As he climbed he put a hand on each thigh. He told the other two what the doctor had told him. As they worked there during the day stripping the tree, they noticed again and again the hollow in the ground where he had been trapped. The fallen leaves there were so dark and wet that it was impossible to distinguish the blood. But every time they noticed the place they questioned whether the doctor could be right.

John Berger   *A Fortunate Man*   1967

One important difference betwen this story by John Berger and the one you have just read by Stuart Hall is that *Crossroads Nowhere* is written from the point of view of the man who is telling the story. This story, on the other hand, is not told from the point of view of any one of the characters involved in the story. We are not drawn into the thoughts and feelings of any character in particular (as we are in *Crossroads Nowhere*). Instead we are given a bird's-eye view of the whole situation. It is not a question of one technique being better than the other: each approach has its strengths and weaknesses, and in your own writing you ought always to think about which approach best suits your subject matter.

1 Summarize clearly what happens in the story.

2 How many people are involved in what happens?

3 If any one character is given more attention than the others, it is the doctor.

   How would you describe his manner on immediately hearing about the accident?

   Why does he keep his 'thumb on the horn'? What does this suggest about his qualities as a doctor?

   Once he has arrived at the scene of the accident, how does he act?

4 How do the woodmen react to the doctor's arrival?

5 Select *two* descriptive details and explain what each detail contributes to the total effect of the story.

6 The accident itself is described very briefly in the first paragraph.

   Why do you think that Berger chooses to write in such short sentences in this paragraph?

   The three verbs used to describe the way in which the man is hit by the tree are 'brushed him down', 'encaged' and 'crushed'.

   In your own words explain exactly what happened, commenting on what each of these verbs tells us about the sequence of events.

   Suppose this paragraph did not exist. Write your own description of the actual accident. Use no more than 200 words and make your description as detailed and realistic as you can.

7 Suppose the story had been written entirely from the point of view of
   a) the injured man
   b) Harry
   c) the doctor

Discuss in each case what might be gained and what lost from the story.

Beginnings

Re-read the first sentence of *Crossroads Nowhere* and the first paragraph of John Berger's story. Berger begins dramatically. His short sentences lead the reader seductively to an understanding of what has happened. We are drawn into the story. Stuart Hall's beginning is not so exciting, but the scene is set: the meaningless, crowded confusion of big-city life is immediately communicated to the reader.

The first sentence and paragraph are important. When looking for a story to read, we usually turn to the beginning. If we like what we read, then we might continue; if the examiner likes your opening sentence, then he, too, might become involved. How you begin a story inevitably sets up expectations in the reader's mind. Consider, for example, the two passages which follow. Each opens a novel. What sort of book would you expect each to be?

> She walked down Fulham Broadway past a shop hung about with cheap underwear, the week-old baby clutched in her arms, his face brick red against his new white bonnet.
>
> Nell Dunn   *Poor Cow* 1967

> A strange melancholy pervades me to which I hesitate to give the grave and beautiful name of sorrow. The idea of sorrow has always appealed to me, but now I am almost ashamed of its complete egoism. I have known boredom, regret, and occasionally remorse, but never sorrow. Today it envelops me like a silken web, enervating and soft, and sets me apart from everybody else.
>
> Francoise Sagan   *Bonjour Tristesse* 1954

As these examples suggest, there are many different ways in which a story can begin. It is, however, possible to make some generalizations about the different *kinds* of opening which are possible.

One technique is to begin with a curious or puzzling statement which is calculated to make the reader interested to know what happens next. Consider these examples:

> I sometimes wonder whether anyone will believe me about this. I don't want to get anyone into trouble but I thought I should just put it down today while it's still fresh. God help me if the superintendent should find these notes though.
>
> Peter Lambley   *Voting Day for Villiers* 1980

Here the opening sentence immediately makes the reader wonder what it is that is going to be revealed. What is the effect of the last sentence which is quoted?

> Around quitting time, Tod Hackett heard a great din on the road
> outside his office. The groan of leather mingled with the jangle of
> iron and over all beat the tattoo of a thousand hooves. He hurried
> to the window.
>
> Nathanael West   *The Day of the Locust*   1939

The technique here is very much the same. Like Tod Hackett, we are
intrigued to know what it is that is making the noise outside the window.

> The naked man lies on the sand spit between the two legs of sea.
> The waves well up the spit and wash the body of the man, who is
> nearly seven feet long. He is prone on his stomach, his face
> turned sideways, his mouth agape with scum running out of his
> gullet to join the backwash of the water. Long strands of seaweed
> foul him, dark as drying blood. One string of rubbery bubbled
> weed winds round his waist and drags back towards the sea. The
> man does not seem to breathe at all.
>
> Andrew Sinclair   *Gog*   1967

Who is this huge, naked man? What has happened to him? Is he alive or
dead? As in the previous examples, this is an opening which fills us with
curiosity. Note, though, that here the writer catches our interest through
his descriptive powers. He does not so much hint at what is to come as
involve us in the mystery right from the start. There is something sinister
about the seaweed, 'dark as drying blood': the phrase hints at an un-
explained violence.

Your own writing

☐ Write an opening sentence or paragraph for stories on each of the following subjects. Make sure that you catch the reader's attention by making
him curious to know what happens next.

> The house on the hill
>
> The accident
>
> A strange present

Beginnings – characters

If one way to begin a story is deliberately to puzzle the reader, another is
immediately to give him information about the characters who will figure
in the story. The aim here is to make the reader interested in the characters, to involve him in their lives so that he wants to read on and find out
more about them.

Mrs Mooney was a butcher's daughter. She was a woman who was quite able to keep things to herself: a determined woman. She had married her father's foreman, and opened a butcher's shop near Spring Gardens. But as soon as his father-in-law was dead Mr Mooney began to go to the devil. He drank, plundered the till, ran headlong into debt. It was no use making him take the pledge: he was sure to break out again a few days after. By fighting his wife in the presence of customers and by buying bad meat he ruined his business. One night he went for his wife with the cleaver, and she had to sleep in a neighbour's house.

After that they lived apart. She went to the priest and got a separation from him, with care of the children. She would give him neither money nor food nor house-room; and so he was obliged to enlist himself as a sheriff's man. He was a shabby stooped little drunkard with a white face and a white moustache and white eyebrows, pencilled above his little eyes, which were pink-veined and raw; and all day long he sat in the bailiff's room, waiting to be put on a job. Mrs Mooney, who had taken what remained of her money out of the butcher business and set up a boarding house in Hardwicke Street, was a big imposing woman. Her house had a floating population made up of tourists from Liverpool and the Isle of Man and, occasionally, *artistes* from the music halls. Its resident population was made up of clerks from the city. She governed the house cunningly and firmly, knew when to give credit, when to be stern and when to let things pass. All the resident young men spoke of her as *The Madam*.

James Joyce   *The Boarding House* from *Dubliners* 1914

A considerable amount of information is compressed into these two paragraphs.

1 What sort of woman is Mrs Mooney?

2 What sort of man is Mr Mooney?

3 What happened between them?

4 What sort of boarding house does Mrs Mooney now run?

Very skilfully, Joyce both tells the reader a great deal about Mr and, in particular, Mrs Mooney, and fills in background information which it is helpful to know before the action of the story begins.

It needs, however, to be emphasized that *The Boarding House* is considerably longer than any story which could be written under examination conditions, and that, since beginning in this way obviously delays the action or main business of the story, you need to think carefully about whether this type of beginning is the best for the story which you are writing. It is very easy to end up with two or three paragraphs of rather boring background information, and no time to write about what is really important.

Your own writing

☐ You are writing a story about someone in their first job. Write the first two paragraphs of the story to introduce the reader to the main character and to the place in which she or he is working.

Beginnings – descriptions

It is also possible to begin a story with a descriptive passage which creates an atmosphere or mood appropriate to the story. The next two passages exemplify this technique.

> Snow covered the airfield.
>
> It had come from the north, in the mist, driven by the night wind, smelling of the sea. There it would stay all Winter, threadbare on the grey earth, an icy, sharp dust; not thawing and freezing, but static like a year without seasons. The changing mist, like the smoke of war, would hang over it, swallow up now a hangar, now the radar hut, now the machines; release them piece by piece, drained of colour, black carrion on a white desert.
>
> It was a scene of no depth, no recession and no shadows. The land was one with the sky; figures and buildings locked in the cold like bodies in an icefloe.
>
> Beyond the airfield there was nothing; no house, no hill, no road; not even a fence, a tree; only the sky pressing on the dunes, the running fog that lifted on the muddy Baltic shore. Somewhere inland were the mountains.
>
> John Le Carré   *The Looking Glass War* 1964

1 How would you describe the atmosphere created in this passage?

2 Which words and phrases seem to you particularly important in creating this atmosphere? Try to explain what it is about these words and phrases which explains the effect that they have.

> The small locomotive engine, Number 4, came clanking, stumbling down from Selston with seven full wagons. It appeared round the corner with loud threats of speed, but the colt that it startled from among the gorse, which still flickered indistinctly in the raw afternoon, out-distanced it at a canter. A woman, walking up the railway line to Underwood, drew back into the hedge, held her basket aside, and watched the footplate of the engine advancing. The trucks thumped heavily past, one by one, with slow inevitable movement, as she stood insignificantly trapped between the jolting black wagons and the hedge; then they curved away towards the coppice where the withered oak leaves dropped noiselessly, while the birds, pulling at the scarlet hips beside the track, made off into the dusk that had already crept

into the spinney. In the open, the smoke from the engine sank and cleaved to the rough grass. The fields were dreary and forsaken, and in the marshy strip that led to the whimsey, a reedy pit-pond, the fowls had already abandoned their run among the adders, to roost in the tarred fowl-house. The pit-bank loomed up beyond the pond, flames like red sores licking its ashy sides, in the afternoon's stagnant light. Just beyond rose the tapering chimneys and the clumsy black headstocks of Brinsley Colliery. The two wheels were spinning fast up against the sky, and the winding engine rapped out its little spasms. The miners were being turned up.

D. H. Lawrence   *Odour of Chrysanthemums* 1914

1 Why does Lawrence make a comparison between the speed of the colt and 'the slow inevitable movement' of the train?
2 Make a list of the adjectives which are used to describe the countryside. Can you make any generalization about their effect?
3 The woman who is 'trapped' between the wagons and the hedge is in fact the main character in the story. What does this first paragraph tell you about her life?

Your own writing

☐ A paragraph of description can lead into a story in an economical and effective way. Write the opening paragraph for stories on the following subjects. Try and make each paragraph create a distinctive atmosphere.

The winter holiday

The party

Blind date

Beginnings – plunging into the action

Finally it is possible to begin a story without any preliminary explanations or scene setting whatsoever. The technique here is to interest the reader in what is actually happening so that he reads on in order to discover more about the people and events he has met on the first page. The next two passages illustrate this technique.

She closed the door behind her, and then it was quite silent, quite dark. She stood, and she could smell very faintly the dry smell of the bracken, coming over the common. Everything was dry now, for three weeks the sun had shone. It tired her. But throughout April and May, it had rained, and that, too, had been tiring, the endless, dull pattering on to the cottage roof. She had not expected to notice, certainly not to be disturbed by, those things –

weather, heat or damp or cloud, night or day, things which existed outside her own self, her own misery. But they had been like burns or abrasions that never healed, irritating her, intruding.

She waited until she could see just a little, and then go down the narrow path between the vegetable beds, and beyond the fruit trees, to where the hens were. There was no sound tonight from the owls in the copse, over to the left of the cottage, no stirring in the trees themselves.

She thought suddenly, I am alone. I am entirely alone on this earth; there are no other people, no animals or birds or insects, no breaths or heartbeats, there is no growing, the leaves do not move and the grass is dry. There is nothing.

And this was a new feeling. No, not a feeling. Loneliness was a feeling, and fear of the empty house and of the long days and nights, and the helpless separation from Ben – feelings. This was different. A condition. A fact. Simply, being absolutely alone.

Then, a cloud slid off the face of the moon, and there was a little light, she could see the grey trunks of the old fruit trees and the bunched tops of the elms. There was no colour, but there were shapes. She began to walk slowly down the garden. It was only nine o'clock. It was the end of August. Each night now, she would put the hens into their coop a few minutes earlier, and those minutes would bring the winter forward. She did not want to think of winter.

Susan Hill   *In the Springtime of the Year* 1974

This passage concentrates on the feelings of a woman whose name we do not yet know. In no more than 100 words summarize what you have learnt from these paragraphs about her situation and emotional state.

The next passage is taken from the opening of *Women in Love*. You are introduced to Ursula and Gudrun Brangwen, two of the main characters in the book. Lawrence does not begin with a description of the two women, but rather lets them reveal something of themselves through their conversation. What they are talking about is their attitude to marriage, and this in itself is significant since much of the book is an account of the relationships which they develop with the men whom they meet.

Ursula and Gudrun Brangwen sat one morning in the window-bay of their father's house in Beldover, working and talking. Ursula was stitching a piece of brightly-coloured embroidery, and Gudrun was drawing upon a board which she held on her knee. They were mostly silent, talking as their thoughts strayed through their minds.

'Ursula,' said Gudrun, 'don't you *really want* to get married?' Ursula laid her embroidery in her lap and looked up. Her face was calm and considerate.

'I don't know,' she replied. 'It depends how you mean.'

Gudrun was slightly taken aback. She watched her sister for some moments.

'Well,' she said, ironically, 'it usually means one thing! But don't you think, anyhow, you'd be –' she darkened slightly – 'in a better position than you are in now.'

A shadow came over Ursula's face.

'I might,' she said. 'But I'm not sure.'

Again Gudrun paused, slightly irritated. She wanted to be quite definite.

'You don't think one needs the *experience* of having been married?' she asked.

'Do you think it need *be* an experience?' replied Ursula.

'Bound to be, in some way or other,' said Gudrun, coolly. 'Possibly undesirable, but bound to be an experience of some sort.'

'Not really,' said Ursula. 'More likely to be the end of experience.'

Gudrun sat very still, to attend to this.

'Of course,' she said, 'there's *that* to consider.' This brought the conversation to a close. Gudrun, almost angrily, took up her rubber and began to rub out part of her drawing. Ursula stitched absorbedly.

'You wouldn't consider a good offer?' asked Gudrun.

'I think I've rejected several,' said Ursula.

'*Really!*' Gundrun flushed dark – 'But anything really worth while? Have you *really*?'

'A thousand a year, and an awfully nice man. I liked him awfully,' said Ursula.

'Really! But weren't you fearfully tempted?

'In the abstract but not in the concrete,' said Ursula. 'When it comes to the point, one isn't even tempted – oh, if I were tempted, I'd marry like a shot. I'm only tempted *not* to.' The faces of both sisters suddenly lit up with amusement.

'Isn't it an amazing thing,' cried Gudrun, 'how strong the temptation is, not to!' They both laughed, looking at each other. In their hearts they were frightened.

D. H. Lawrence   *Women in Love* 1921

1 In no more than 80 words summarize what is said about marriage.

2 What impression do you form of the two sisters from this conversation?

3 What is the effect of the last sentence?

Your own writing

To be successful this kind of beginning needs both to interest the reader so that he will wish to read on and to present him with information which is important to the story. Susan Hill tells us about the emotional state of her main character; Lawrence introduces the theme of marriage.

☐ Suppose you are writing a story about a girl who has discovered that her boyfriend is stealing from his work so that he has enough money to take her out. Write the first paragraph or so of this story so that the reader is plunged into the story without any introduction. You can do this in one of three ways:

by writing, like Susan Hill, an account of the girl's or boy's feelings.

by writing, like Lawrence, a conversation between the boy and the girl about his stealing.

by making up a scene which is in some way relevant to the subject of the story: a scene, for instance, in which the boy is shown stealing, or in which the girl finds out about what he is doing.

Shaping a story

In the previous section of this chapter you studied the different ways in which it is possible to begin a story. In fact, of course, it is difficult to decide how to begin until you have some sense of the shape or form of the whole story. What exactly is going to happen in your story? How will it end? How do you want the reader to feel on finishing the story? These are some of the questions you need to think about in planning any story which you write.

Read the following story and answer the questions set on it. These questions are designed to make you think about how this story has been constructed and, more generally, about what is involved in writing stories which are tightly and coherently structured.

"Where you' father?"

The boy did not answer. He paddled his boat carefully between the shallows, and then he ran the boat alongside the bank, putting his paddle in front to stop it. Then he threw the rope round the picket and helped himself on to the bank. His mother stood in front of the door still staring at him.

"Where you' father?"

The boy disguised his irritation. He looked at his mother and said calmly, "You know Pa. You know where he is."

"And ah did tell you not to come back without 'im?"

"I could bring Pa back?" The boy cried. His bitterness was getting the better of him. "When Pa want to drink I could bring him back?"

It was always the same. The boy's mother stood in front of the door staring up the river. Every Saturday night it was like this. Every Saturday night Mano went out to the village and drank himself helpless and lay on the floor of the shop, cursing and vomiting until the Chinaman was ready to close up. Then they rolled him outside and heaven knows, maybe they even spat on him.

The boy's mother stared up the river, her face twisted with anger and distress. She couldn't go up the river now. It would be hell and fire if she went. But Mano had to be brought home. She turned to see what the boy was doing. He had packed away the things from the shopping bag and he was now reclining on the settee.

"You have to go for you' father, you know," she said.

"Who?"

"You!"

"Not me!"

"Who de hell you tellin' not me," she shouted. She was furious now. "Dammit, you have to go for you' father!"

Sona had risen from the settee on the alert. His mother hardly ever hit him now but he could never tell. It had been a long time since she had looked so angry and had stamped her feet.

He rose slowly and reluctantly and as he glanced at her he couldn't understand what was wrong with her. He couldn't see why she bothered about his father at all. For his father was stupid and worthless and made their life miserable. If he could have had his way Mano would have been out of the house a long time now. His bed would have been the dirty meat-table in front of Assing's shop. That was what he deserved. The rascal! The boy spat through the window. The very thought of his father sickened him.

Yet with Sona's mother it was different. The man she had married and who had turned out badly was still the pillar of her life. Although he had piled up grief after grief, tear after tear, she felt lost and drifting without him. To her he was as mighty as the very Ortoire that flowed outside. She remembered that in his young days there was nothing any living man could do that he could not.

In her eyes he was still young. He did not grow old. It was she who had aged. He had only turned out badly. She hated him for the way he drank rum and squandered the little money he worked for. But she did not mind the money so much. It was seeing him drunk. She knew when he arrived back staggering how she would shake with rage and curse him, but even so, how inside she would shake with the joy of having him safe and home.

She wondered what was going on at the shop now. She wondered if he was already drunk and helpless and making a fool of himself.

With Sona, the drunkard's son, this was what stung more than ever. The way Mano, his father, cursed everybody and made a fool of himself. Sometimes he had listened to his father and he had felt to kick him, so ashamed he was. Often in silence he had shaken his fist and said, "One day, ah'll – ah'll . . ."

He had watched his mother put up with hell and sweat and starvation. She was getting skinnier every day, and she looked more like fifty-six than the thirty-six she was. Already her hair was greying. Sometimes he had looked at her and, thinking of his father, he had ground his teeth and had said, "Beast!" several times to himself. He was in that frame of mind now. Bitter and reluctant, he went to untie the boat.

"If I can't bring 'im, I'll leave 'im," he said angrily.

"Get somebody to help you!"

He turned to her. "Nobody wouldn't help me. He does insult everybody. Last week Bolai kick him."

"Bolai kick 'im? An' what you do?"

His mother was stung with rage and shock. Her eyes were large and red and watery.

The boy casually unwound the rope from the picket. "What I do?" he said. "That is he and Bolai business."

His mother burst out crying.

"What ah must do?" the boy said. "All the time ah say, 'Pa, come home, come home, Pa!' You know what he tell me? He say, 'Go to hell, yuh little bitch!'"

His mother turned to him. Beads of tears were still streaming down the sides of her face.

"Sona, go for you' father. Go now. You stand up dey and watch Bolai kick you' father and you ent do nothing? He mind you, you know," she sobbed. "He is you' father, you ungrateful –" And choking with anger and grief she burst out crying again.

When she raised her head, Sona was paddling towards mid-stream, scowling, avoiding the shallows of the river.

True enough there was havoc in Assing's shop. Mano's routine was well under way. He staggered about the bar dribbling and cursing and yet again the Chinaman spoke to him about his words, not that he cared about Mano's behaviour. The rum Mano consumed made quite a difference to Assing's account. It safe-guarded Mano's free speech in the shop.

But the customers were disgusted. All sorts of things had happened on Saturday nights through Mano's drunkenness. There was no such thing as buying in peace once Mano was there.

So now with trouble looming, the coming of Sona was sweet relief. As Sona walked in, someone pointed out his father between the sugar bags.

"Pa!"

Mano looked up. "What you come for?" he drawled. "Who send you?"

"Ma say to come home," Sona said. He told himself that he mustn't lose control in front of strangers.

"Well!"

"Ma send me for you."

"You! You' mother send you for me! So you is me father now, eh – eh?" In his drunken rage the old man staggered towards his son.

Sona didn't walk back. He never did anything that would make him feel stupid in front of a crowd. But before he realised what was happening his father lunged forward and struck him on his left temple.

"So you is me father, eh? You is me father, now!" He kicked the boy.

Two or three people bore down on Mano and held him off the boy. Sona put his hands to his belly where his father had just kicked him. Tears came to his eyes. The drunkenness was gripping Mano more and more. He could hardly stand on his own now. He was struggling to set himself free. The men held on to him. Sona kept out of the way.

"It's a damn' shame!" somebody said.

"Shame?" Mano drawled. "An' he is me father now, 'e modder send him for me. Let me go," he cried, struggling more than ever, "I'll kill 'im. So help me God, I'll kill 'im!"

They hadn't much to do to control Mano at this stage. His body was supple and weak now, as if his bones were turning to water. The person who had cried, "It's a damn' shame!" spoke again.

"Why you don't carry 'im home, boy? You can't see 'e only making botheration?"

"You'll help me put 'im in the boat?" Sona asked. He looked unruffled now. He seemed only concerned with getting his father out of the shop, and out of all this confusion. Nobody could tell what went on below the calmness of his face. Nobody could guess that hate was blazing in his mind.

Four men and Sona lifted Mano and carted him into the boat. The old man was snoring, in a state of drunkenness. It was the state of drunkenness when things were at rest.

The four men pushed the boat off. Sona looked at his father. After a while he looked back at the bridge. Everything behind was swallowed by the darkness. "Pa," the boy said. His father groaned. "Pa, yuh going home," Sona said.

The wilderness of mangroves and river spread out before the boat. They were alone. Sona was alone with Mano, and the river and the mangroves and the night, and the swarms of alligators below. He looked at his father again. "Pa, so you kick me up then, eh?" he said.

Far into the night Sona's mother waited. She slept a little on one side, then she turned on the other side, and at every sound she woke up, straining her ears. There was no sound of the paddle on water. Surely the shops must have closed by now, she thought. Everything must have closed by this time. She lay there anxious and listened until her eyes shut again in an uneasy sleep.

She was awakened by the creaking of the bedroom floor. Sona jumped back when she spoke.

"Who that – Mano?"

"Is me, Ma," Sona said.

His bones, too, seemed to be turning liquid. Not from drunkenness, but from fear. The lion in him had changed into a lamb. As he spoke his voice trembled.

His mother didn't notice. "All you now, come?" she said. "Where Mano?"

The boy didn't answer. In the darkness he took down his things from the nails.

"Where Mano?" his mother cried out.

"He out there sleeping. He drunk."

"The bitch!" his mother said, getting up and feeling for the matches.

Sona quickly slipped outside. Fear dazed him now and he felt dizzy. He looked at the river and he looked back at the house and there was only one word that kept hitting against his mind: Police!

"Mano!" he heard his mother call to the emptiness of the house. "Mano!"

Panic-stricken, Sona fled into the mangroves and into the night.

Michael Anthony   *Drunkard of the River*   1960

1 This story, though short, divides into three separate scenes. What are these scenes?

2 What do we learn in the first scene about:

the boy's feelings towards his father?

his feelings towards his mother?

her feelings towards her husband?

This scene prepares us for the next stage of the story. It is necessary for us to know about what the boy feels so that we can understand why he acts as he does later in the story.

3 What does Mano do to Sona in the shop?

4 How does Sona behave? What is he in fact feeling under the surface?

5 The second scene ends with Sona's words to his father: 'Pa, so you kick me up then, eh?' We are not actually told what happens next. Why do you think that Michael Anthony chooses not to describe what is in a sense the most important event in the story?

6 What are Sona's feelings in the last scene?

7 Sona is the only character who figures in each scene, and it is largely through his eyes that we view what happens. How do you think we are meant to feel about Sona and what he does?

8 Although it is true to say that Sona is the central character, we in fact learn quite a lot in the first scene about how his mother feels about his father. How does this knowledge affect your reaction to what happens?

Answering these questions should have made you realize how carefully the story has been planned or 'shaped'. There is the division into three scenes, and the way each scene leads into the next. In particular there is the calculated decision not to describe the actual murder. There is the fact that Sona is clearly the most important character. Think about how the story could have been told in different ways, of how, for instance, the boy could have been made to seem more brutal, the father more pathetic, and so on. What Michael Anthony has done is to decide the general effect he wants the story to have, and how he wants each character to appear. This careful planning underlies any good story, and it is what you should be aiming for in your own writing.

Endings

Endings, like beginnings, are important and often difficult. They are difficult because everything in the story has to be tied up neatly, but if this bringing together is *too* neat then it will seem artificial and contrived. We want to believe in the stories we read, to feel that they are like life, and life, unlike stories, tends to go on in a rather inconclusive way.

Think again about the last sentence of *Drunkard of the River*: 'Panic-stricken, Sona fled into the mangroves and the night'. This makes a highly satisfying end to the story precisely because although his flight is a neat point on which to end the story we have a sense of his life going on. We wonder as we stop reading what is going to happen to him, whether he will see his mother again, whether he will be caught and tried as a murderer, or what.

It is obviously difficult to think about the ending of a story unless you know the story which has gone before. Read, however, the following passages to gain some sense of how different writers have solved the problem of bringing their stories to a satisfactory conclusion.

One obvious technique is to have the central character die, or, as in this example from a writer who, like Michael Anthony, comes from the Caribbean, be killed. The danger with this technique is that it can often seem melodramatic and rather too obvious. This particular passage avoids these dangers through the sensitive and moving way in which Enrique Serpa analyses the dying man's thoughts.

> The dry crack of a shot disturbed the morning quiet. Felipe without understanding how or why suddenly felt himself stopped. Then he slumped down on the water-front, his eyes gazing at the sky. Against the limpid blue, he saw a long, shining cloud. "Like mother of pearl," he thought. And he remembered

with extraordinary clarity the delicate sea-shells which decorated his childhood years. Some were perfectly white, others a more tender colour, a marvellous pale pink. He had lots of shells which he kept in boxes, mostly old shoe-boxes. "And now I must buy shoes for the kids because they are going around barefoot." This thought brought him back to reality. In a giddy succession of images he remembered his quarrel with the policeman. Did he actually hit him? An unspeakable lassitude, a sort of pleasant tiredness and feeling of comfort were relaxing his muscles. Suddenly he realised that he was dying. It was not lassitude or tiredness or comfort, it was his life leaving him. But he did not want to die, he could not die. It was his duty not to die. What would happen to his children? He must defend his life which was the life of his children, defend it with his hands, his feet, his teeth. His mouth was dumb as if it were already full of earth. But he was not dead yet. He tried to form a clear image of his children, but it kept slipping away, blurred and fleeting. In the distance, as if from miles away, he heard Congo's voice. Another voice. Other voices. He could not get the picture of his children clear. He could make out a vague, hazy outline as in a bad photograph. His heavy eyelids gradually closed. His mouth twisted in a desperate effort to speak. At last he was able to murmur: "My children . . . my . . . my . . ."

He trembled violently and then remained motionless and silent, still and mute, his eyes staring at the sky.

On his chest over the left breast, almost invisible, there was a small red hole, about the size of a five-cent piece.

Enrique Serpa   *Shark Fins*

1 What is the man pre-occupied by?

2 Can you pin-point what it is in the writing that explains its emotional impact?

This second example is the ending of Paul Theroux's novel, *The Family Arsenal*. Like Michael Anthony, Theroux leaves the reader with a feeling that though the story has stopped the lives of the characters go on.

'Put your feet up,' said Murf. 'Get the benefit. I wish Brodie was here. She likes a good train ride.' He took out his marking crayon and smiled at the wall.

Hood said, 'Don't.'

'I wasn't really going to.' He put the crayon away.

'You didn't have to come.'

'I'm sticking wif you.'

'It might not be what you think.'

'Yeah. Even if it ain't, I'm sticking.' He fumbled in the pocket of his jacket and took out his leather stash, his cigarette papers. He began rolling a cigarette.

Hood said, 'You'll be all right.'

'Yeah.'

Hood put his feet up, on the seat opposite.

'That's the idea,' said Murf. 'Get the benefit.' He licked the cigarette, giving it the colour of his tongue. 'But I mean, where are we really going?'

'Guatemala.'

'Yeah.'

Jason, sniffing the strong smoke, made a face at Murf. He said nothing. He turned again to the window. Hood sorrowed for his small pathetic neck.

Murf said, 'Yeah, but what'll we do when we get there?'

Hood nodded slowly and took Murf's cigarette. He puffed it, handed it back and put his hands behind his head. The sun striped the compartment with heat; the horn blew again, long and sad, but the train sped them away from its stuttering echo.

'Smoke', he said. Then, 'Smoke and tell lies.'

Paul Theroux   *The Family Arsenal* 1976

☐ Comment on the effect of the last sentence.

A third way in which a story can be ended is with a descriptive passage which creates an atmosphere that is relevant to what has happened in the story.

The farmhouse lay in darkness, blind and not hearing, motionless against the swaying larches and the running sky.

They had left a shutter open and it banged slowly without rhythm, according to the strength of the storm. Snow gathered like ash and was dispersed. They had gone, leaving nothing behind them but tyre tracks in the hardening mud, a twist of wire, and the sleepless tapping of the north wind.

John Le Carré   *The Looking Glass War* 1964

1 What kind of atmosphere is created here?

2 Can you make any guesses about the kind of story which this might have been?

This next passage is an example of an ending which seems much more conclusive and final in that the narrator is analysing the experiences which have led him to this point in his life. It needs, however, to be said that even in this passage there is a sense of a new future opening even though the story has ended.

I was leaving the South to fling myself into the unknown, to meet other situations that would perhaps elicit from me other responses. And if I could meet enough of a different life, then, perhaps, gradually and slowly I might learn who I was, what I might be. I was not leaving the South to forget the South, but so that some day I might understand it, might come to know what its rigours had done to me, to its children. I fled so that the numbness of my defensive living might thaw out and let me feel the pain – years later and far away – of what living in the South had meant.

Yet, deep down, I knew that I could never really leave the South, for my feelings had already been formed by the South, for there had been slowly instilled into my personality and consciousness, black though I was, the culture of the South. So, in leaving, I was taking a part of the South to transplant in alien soil, to see if it could grow differently, if it could drink of new and cool rains, bend in strange winds, respond to the warmth of other suns, and, perhaps, to bloom. . . . And if that miracle ever happened, then I would know that there was yet hope in that Southern swamp of despair and violence, that light could emerge even out of the blackest of the southern night. I would know that the South too could overcome its fear, its hate, its cowardice, its heritage of guilt and blood, its burden of anxiety and compulsive cruelty.

With ever watchful eyes and bearing scars, visible and invisible, I headed North, full of a hazy notion that life could be lived with dignity, that the personalities of others should not be violated, that men should be able to confront other men without fear or shame, and that if men were lucky in their living on earth they might win some redeeming meaning for their having struggled and suffered here beneath the stars.

Richard Wright   *Black Boy* 1974

This is a novel about the childhood and youth of a black boy in the South of the USA.

1 What reasons does the narrator give in this passage for leaving the South?
2 Why does he feel that he can never really escape from the South?
3 What does he feel is wrong with the South?
4 What conclusions can you draw about the narrator's personality from this passage?
5 Would you describe this as an optimistic ending, or not?

Your own writing

☐ Write appropriate endings to stories in which:

a child has been wrongly punished for something which he/she did not do two friends have been rescued from a cave in which they have been lost for three days

a young teacher has experienced a great deal of difficulty in controlling a third-year class.

The work you have done in earlier sections of this chapter has, of course, involved you in thinking about how you can write better stories of your own. The advice given here summarizes the comments which have already been made.

☐ Keep the story simple. It is not necessary to have a complicated or violent plot in order to interest the reader, and it might well be a good idea to focus on just one event.

☐ Write about what you know. If you have first-hand experience of your subject matter then your writing is likely to be convincing; if you lack this experience then the chances are that what you write will fail to ring true.

☐ Come to a clear decision about what you really want the story to say. Who is going to be the most important character? What will be the main event? How do you want the reader to feel after he or she has finished the story? Only when you have thought about these questions can you decide how to shape the story to maximum effect.

☐ Try and involve the reader in your first sentence or paragraph.

☐ End the story in as memorable a way as you can.

The list which follows contains ideas for writing stories. While you will obviously not write stories which develop each of these ideas, you would do well to think about how you might plan several of them.

Write a story:

a) in which an accident happens

b) about trouble at a disco

c) told from the point of view of an old person who has been caught shoplifting

d) in which a friendship breaks up

e) about a boy or girl who moves to a new school at the end of the fourth year

f) which depends for its effect largely on descriptive detail about a quarrel and which makes considerable use of conversation

g) about an important family decision and written by a narrator who reveals how each member of the family feels about the decision

h) about something ludicrous or embarrassing and which is written in the first person

i) in which someone alone in a house is terrified by an intruder

Chapter Four

Practical writing

A distinction was made in the introduction to this book between imaginative and practical writing. So far you have studied passages which illustrate some of the most important techniques involved in writing imaginatively. This chapter concentrates on practical writing: on writing summaries (or précis, as they are sometimes called), explanations and instructions, letters and reports. You might well be asked in the examination to make a summary of a longer piece of writing, or to write a business letter, or a report based on your interpretation of evidence given to you. These are skills, moreover, which are essential to many jobs in the outside world. So it is important that you understand what is involved in each of these different types of writing. In this chapter you will find examples of each type, advice on how to tackle the kinds of question often set in the examination, and writing exercises designed to help you practise the skills you have learnt.

Writing a summary

Most language examinations contain a question which asks the candidate to summarize either part or all of a passage. The precise form which this question takes varies from Board to Board, but, whatever the exact wording of the question, you should always approach a summary in the same way. In the following pages you will learn how to do this, and you will have the opportunity to develop your skill in summarizing through tackling a number of different types of summary question.

Summarizing a story or an argument is not just something that you have to do in an English examination. In everyday life we often perform exactly the same task. Telling a friend about a book which we have read involves us in selecting what is important from the book so that the friend can understand what it is about. To do this successfully we need *both* a firm sense of what happens in the book *and* the ability to express this knowledge in a fluent and concise way. This is equally true of the examination exercise: *a summary question is a test of your ability to understand the original passage and of your skill in expressing this understanding in a clear and logical fashion.*

For obvious reasons, short passages are generally easier to summarize than longer and more complicated pieces of writing. The following passages are, therefore, included to help you understand what is involved in writing a summary.

☐ Read each passage and summarize the main point which is made in *one sentence*. As far as is possible, use your own words.

FARM BUILDINGS are as much a part of our ideal view of the countryside as woods, meadows and churches. It is difficult to imagine an "English" landscape without a barn in it.

Yet most of them are lingering in borrowed time. As the principal working building on the farm, the traditional barn was built only with the finest local timber or stone – so solidly, in fact, that many of them have outlived their usefulness. Early in the 19th century, their main functions of storing and processing corn were usurped by the rickyard and the threshing machine. Many farms have adapted them to other purposes – processing animal feed, for instance, or for storage. But others have knocked them down or allowed them to decay.

Sunday Times 2.11.80

All the evidence shows that in Western society no adequate substitute has been found for the one-to-one, warm, continuous, loving and mutually enjoyable relationship which is the essence of maternal care. This is particularly so during the earliest years of life. However, that does not mean that the same person must provide uninterrupted care for 24 hours a day. Quite the reverse. It is wise to accustom even quite young babies to being looked after by someone else for short periods . . .

It is very difficult to meet these needs by providing substitute care, since most available options have serious shortcomings. Even at best, they rarely provide adequate, consistent mothering or stimulating new experiences. Their most harmful impact is on the child's emotional and intellectual development . . .

In short, only the very rich or the very lucky have access to satisfactory full-time, daily substitute care. To provide a high quality system would be very costly and take years to develop. In any case, is this really the best way ahead? Is not full-time mothering for young children a preferable choice and in the interest of mothers themselves?

Mia Kellmer-Pringle *Half the Sky*

"DEAR JOHN," my solicitor writes to me. "Dear John," writes my accountant. "Dear John," writes the architect who planned the conversion of the cottage I half-own. "Dear John," writes the builder who carried out the work. "Dear John," writes the friend's child, aged eight, thanking me in big, straggly characters for a birthday present.

No, I am not complaining. It is friendly and egalitarian and modern. I like them all, and I would not want them to address me as "Dear Sir", or "Dear Mr Townsend." This is the age of Instant First Names. Anything more formal sounds stilted.

And yet . . . when everyone speaks and writes in the vocabulary of intimacy, is there not a sense in which intimacy ceases to exist? When everybody you meet talks to you from the beginning like a dear old friend, is there a risk that you are not quite sure who your real friends are?

John Townsend
Sunday Times 14.12.80

Think of Mrs Armstrong as you pull your Christmas crackers this year. She could be any one of dozens of one-parent families on any social worker's caseload, or another hopeless transfer case on the files in a local housing department. As it happens, she is married – to a low-paid worker – and lives in a council flat in Kent.

Three young children mean that she can't go out to work. So she assembles Christmas crackers for a novelty firm. The spirit of Christmas is entirely absent from the tireless chore of working 36 hours a week for a gross wage of only £5 or £6 – or just 96p for every dozen boxes of twelve crackers.

Not all Britain's 150,000 to 250,000 homeworkers are young mothers, though they (single or married to a low-paid or unemployed worker) make up the vast majority of a workforce for whom the living room acts as a sweat shop and warehouse: their own poverty trap. The long-term sick, women looking after infirm relatives, immigrant wives, families in the more remote rural communities, all are prime candidates for similar exploitation, as the latest report of the Low Pay Unit makes plain (*The Hidden Army. New Society*, 20.12.79

Across all sections of society it has been normal to regard the boy as the bread winner and the girl as the future mother, deputising for the mother when circumstances so demand. Boys appear more likely to be encouraged in the direction of higher and further education than are girls: more encouraged also to gain specific qualifications. In general parents are likely to show more concern about the future economic prospects of their sons than they do about those of their daughters. There are indications, however, that attitudes are changing. A number of head teachers have declared that many parents regard the employment prospects of girls and boys as of equal importance.
Curricular Differences for Boys and Girls, DES, quoted in *Half The Sky*

The passages which you have just summarized were probably short enough for you to read and hold in your mind without too much difficulty. The problem you will be faced with in summarizing a longer passage is that the writer will often make a number of points in support of his main argument. If this is the case then your summary ought to contain the most important of these points. It ought, in other words, to reflect the way in which the argument is developed in the original passage. Most people find that they cannot remember the original clearly enough without making some notes as they go along. You are therefore recommended to follow this procedure in summarizing longer and more complicated passages.

Stage 1
Read the original passage fairly quickly in order to gain a general impression of what it is about.

Stage 2
In order to see if you have grasped what it is basically about, try at this stage to find a short title which sums up the essential point being made.

Stage 3
Now go through the passage paragraph by paragraph, and briefly note down how the argument is developed.

Stage 4
Write a rough draft of your summary from these notes. Evidence which is quoted in the original passage in support of the argument made should only be included if you have any words left over after summarizing the actual argument. Use your own words as far as is possible.

Stage 5
Compare your draft to the original passage to see if you have left out anything important.

Stage 6
Write the final version, improving the style of the draft in any way that you can.

Clearly, if you are only asked to summarize part of a passage or if there are particular instructions which you are given, then you will vary your approach accordingly. *It is always, however, worth remembering these instructions as the standard way of approaching a summary exercise.*

The following question is an example of a traditional summary exercise. Underneath the passage are printed notes and a possible version of the final summary. Study these notes and the summary so that you are sure you understand what is involved in tackling this sort of question.

Write a summary of the following passage in good continuous prose, using not more than 120 words. State at the end of the summary the number of words you have used. The passage contains 348 words. (16 marks)

As Britain's social services have rapidly extended their scope, they have, whilst attempting to solve urgent social problems, created new perplexities. One of the great difficulties in organizing a service intended to include the whole community is that it may be too impersonal, employing, as it must, thousands of people in its huge administrative machine. It is often difficult for the individual whom the service is designed to help to receive the personal attention and interest which seem so important to him in his time of trouble. The application for benefit is made even more impersonal by the necessity to fill in forms, a task which the average person finds difficult and often distasteful; not all the details required are intelligible to the applicant. If a man is seriously injured on his way home from work and taken to hospital, his harassed wife, still recovering from the shock, is faced with form-filling which requires tremendous efforts of memory, a detailed knowledge of her incapacitated husband's affairs and a capacity to answer formal questions beyond the skill even of people who are not suffering from shock. Then comes the waiting for the mysterious processes of reception, verification and certification to be completed in some unknown office, before benefit can be awarded or any result disclosed.

There is now evidence of a move by the Department of Social Security to make its officers aware of the social and human problems arising from distress and hardship and of the principles involved in establishing good feelings between civil servants and applicants for benefit. Indeed, officers are given facilities to attend specially designed courses at extra-mural departments of some universities, where they are helped to understand the complex and delicate task of dealing with persons in need. It is difficult to assess the extent to which this enlightened approach has been successful in making the social services truly personal, but from discussions with those who dispense and those who receive benefits, it seems clear that there is now a different attitude from that of the awesome Poor Law administrators of the not-so-distant past.

D. Marsh (adapted)
AEB Ordinary Level English Language Syllabus I June 1977

This summary has been written by the author and has not been endorsed by the Associated Examining Board.

Stage 2

A title for this passage might be: 'A Humane Approach to Social Distress'.

Stage 3

Paragraph One: Expansion of social services has caused new problems.

Problem of impersonality

Need to make people feel that there is personal concern.

Problem of form-filling and waiting for the results of applications - ~~cause eg. the wife whose husband has been hurt returning from work~~.

Paragraph Two: Department of Social Security is trying to
educate its officers toward an understanding
of the need for good human relationships.
University courses
Some evidence of improvement.

Stage 4

~~Britain's social services have~~ been ~~expanded to~~ deal ~~create~~ with
~~pressing problems~~. The expansion of Britain's social
services has ~~caused~~ created new difficulties. ~~When many people are~~
~~employed~~ X one major problem is that the larger the service,
the more ~~remote~~ impersonal it becomes. ~~Individuals~~ People in ~~distress~~ trouble
need personal ~~help,~~ attention X ~~Many of the forms which have~~
~~to be filled in~~ and administrative procedures which
involve complicated form-filling and long periods of
waiting for the results of applications cause ~~worse~~ further
~~unhappiness~~ distress suffering to distressed or shocked claimants.

~~The Department of Social Security now seems aware~~
~~of this problem~~ The Department of Social Security
~~now~~ seems, however, to be trying to make its officers
~~appreciate~~ understand' that ~~they should~~ it is necessary to respond to
applicants for benefit ~~as people with problems~~ as human
beings in distress. Officers are, for instance, ~~encouraged~~ attending
encouraged to attend special university courses to ~~help~~
~~them understand~~ study these problems. ~~How successful~~
~~these courses have been we do not yet know It is~~
Although it is difficult to judge ~~whether~~ the success
of these innovations, it seems that attitudes are
changing for the better.

93

Stage 6

The expansion of Britain's social services has created new difficulties. One major problem is that the larger the service, the more impersonal it becomes. People in trouble need personal attention. Administrative procedures which involve complicated form filling and long periods of waiting for the results of applications cause further suffering to distressed or shocked claimants.

The Department of Social Security seems, however, to be trying to make its officers understand that it is necessary to respond to applicants for benefit as human beings in distress. Officers are, for instance, encouraged to. attending special university courses to study these problems. Although it is difficult to judge the success of these innovations, it seems that attitudes are changing for the better.

Total words used. 119

Now practise this approach to the writing of summaries. The questions which follow represent the different kinds of summary exercise which you might face in the examination. The first questions are easier than the later ones.

1 *The following extract is taken from an article in the 'Reader's Digest' of October 1975 entitled 'Private Shame for Two Million Britons'. It is about the problem of adult illiteracy.*

Read the extract carefully and then answer the questions which follow.

How is it possible for a boy or girl to go into the world unable to read after nine or ten years of compulsory education? There are scores of reasons: schooling interrupted by frequent illness, undetected eyesight or hearing troubles, personal antagonism to teachers, unhappy home backgrounds. Educationalists criticize new – and old – methods of teaching reading, over-large classes, unskilled teachers, too much attention to bright pupils at the expense of the slow. Many middle-aged illiterates blame wartime evacuation to the country, where overworked teachers had no time to help children emotionally upset through separation from their parents.

Home backgrounds are an all important factor. The dice are unfairly loaded against the child whose illiterate parents are incapable of stimulating his interest by reading to him. Unfamiliar with the very sight of books, he starts school at a disadvantage, and soon lags behind other children who learned the pleasure of the printed word at their mother's knee. Even if he does learn to read hesitantly, he may quickly forget when he leaves school because there's nothing to read at home.

Fear of losing face haunts those who cannot read. Some buy a newspaper every morning, wishing to look like their workmates, yet hesitate to open it in case somebody asks about a story inside. The customer in the post office who produces broken spectacles, and apologetically asks you to fill in his form, may habitually carry them for such situations. The bandaged hand is another variation.

Broadcasting may be the solution. A great step forward will come this month (October 1975) when the BBC reaches out to illiterates in the privacy of their own homes with a three-year series of radio and television programmes, which will encourage them to seek help and at the same time give basic teaching. It is the most ambitious literacy project ever mounted in a developed Western country.

Level One, the first year-long series of 50 television programmes, will show adults talking freely about their reading difficulties and explain how to get information about local tuition without embarrassment. Assuming viewers will be completely illiterate, the series will guide them through the earliest reading steps, including how to recognize letters, and teach useful everyday 'sign' words such as 'Ladies' and 'Gentlemen'.

Level Two, reinforced with radio readings, will begin in a year's time to develop the skills learned in Level One, and both will be repeated in 1977. Each programme will give viewers the telephone number of a referral service, whose staff will take down and pass on details to a local education authority for action. Co-operation is the Literacy Agency's campaign code word. As Director Bill Devereux says, 'We aim to maximize all the local and national resources available.'

Success will create a new problem: where to find the tutors. Thousands of volunteers are being recruited and trained to help professionals cope with the expected response, but many more are needed. This is where the rest of us can give positive and personal help. Anyone who is literate is a potential teacher. Basic training can be gained in six lessons, and BBC Radio Three is to broadcast eight instructional programmes for prospective tutors.

In answering these questions you MUST use your own words as far as is possible. MARKS WILL BE DEDUCTED IF YOU DO NOT DO THIS.

a) List SEVEN of the reasons given in the first paragraph for inability to read. Write them each on a separate line. Be as brief as possible.

b) In no more than 30 words summarize what is said about the importance of home background in the second paragraph. Write in sentences.

c) In no more than 25 words say how illiteracy is embarrassing to people. (Third paragraph). Write in sentences.

d) Using the information in the last four paragraphs, and using no more than 60 words, summarize what is said about the broadcasts to help illiterates. You may use note form as long as your notes are something more than odd phrases strung together.

West Midlands Examination Board C.S.E. English Studies, Paper II, May, 1977.

2   An old man with steel rimmed spectacles and very dusty clothes
       sat by the side of the road. There was a pontoon bridge across the
       river and carts, trucks, and men, women and children were
       crossing it. The mule-drawn carts staggered up the steep bank
5   from the bridge with soldiers helping push against the spokes of
       the wheels. The trucks ground up and away heading out of it all
       and the peasants plodded along in the ankle deep dust. But the
       old man sat there without moving. He was too tired to go any
       farther.
10   It was my business to cross the bridge, explore the bridgehead
       beyond and find out to what point the enemy had advanced. I did
       this and returned over the bridge. There were not so many carts
       now and very few people on foot, but the old man was still there.
           "Where do you come from?" I asked him.
15   "From San Carlos," he said, and smiled.
           That was his native town and so it gave him pleasure to
       mention it and he smiled.
           "I was taking care of animals," he explained.
           "Oh," I said, not quite understanding.
20   "Yes," he said, "I stayed, you see, taking care of animals. I
       was the last one to leave the town of San Carlos."
           He did not look like a shepherd nor a herdsman and I looked
       at his black dusty clothes and his gray dusty face and his steel
       rimmed spectacles and said, "What animals were they?"
25   "Various animals," he said, and shook his head. "I had to leave
       them."
           I was watching the bridge and the African looking country of
       the Ebro Delta and wondering how long now it would be before
       we would see the enemy, and listening all the while for the first
30   noises that would signal that ever mysterious event called con-
       tact, and the old man still sat there.
           "What animals were they?" I asked.
           "There were three animals altogether," he explained. "There
       were two goats and a cat and then there were four pairs of
35   pigeons."
           "And you had to leave them?" I asked.

"Yes. Because of the artillery. The captain told me to go because of the artillery."

"And you have no family?" I asked, watching the far end of
40 the bridge where a few last carts were hurrying down the slope of the bank.

"No," he said, "only the animals I stated. The cat, of course, will be all right. A cat can look out for itself, but I cannot think what will become of the others."

45 "What politics have you?" I asked.

"I am without politics," he said. "I am seventy-six years old. I have come twelve kilometers now and I think now I can go no further."

"This is not a good place to stop," I said. "If you can make it,
50 there are trucks up the road where it forks for Tortosa."

"I will wait a while," he said, "and then I will go. Where do the trucks go?"

"Towards Barcelona," I told him.

"I know no one in that direction," he said, "but thank you
55 very much. Thank you again very much."

He looked at me very blankly and tiredly, then said, having to share his worry with some one, "The cat will be all right, I am sure. There is no need to be unquiet about the cat. But the others. Now what do you think about the others?"

60 "Why, they'll probably come through it all right."

"You think so?"

"Why not?" I said, watching the far bank where now there were no carts.

"But what will they do under the artillery when I was told to
65 leave because of the artillery?"

"Did you leave the dove cage unlocked?" I asked.

"Yes."

"Then they'll fly."

"Yes, certainly they'll fly. But the others. It's better not to
70 think about the others," he said.

"If you are rested I would go," I urged. "Get up and try to walk now."

"Thank you," he said and got to his feet, swayed from side to side and then sat down backwards in the dust.

75 "I was taking care of animals," he said dully, but no longer to me.

"I was only taking care of animals."

There was nothing to do about him. It was Easter Sunday and the Fascists were advancing towards the Ebro. It was a grey
80 overcast day with a low ceiling so their planes were not up. That and the fact that cats know how to look after themselves was all the good luck that old man would ever have.

Turn over for the question related to this passage.

Write a description of the old man, concentrating particularly on his state of mind. About 120 words should be enough.

Metropolitan Regional Examination Board, Paper I, 1979

3 The passage below is part of an introduction to a book containing some of the early scripts used in a television series called *Z Cars*. Read it carefully and then answer the questions that follow.

Television is an electronic way of carrying words and pictures from one place to another. At its best it meets a need. It can bring to medical students a close-up picture of an operation that they could not otherwise see, it allows the police to observe traffic jams and plot ways out of them, and it can bring to a large audience national events and news which affect the whole nation.

Nobody needs hour after hour of television, yet to justify their existence and pay their way, the television companies have to make themselves needed. This they can only do by encouraging the habit of viewing; the theory is that once a viewing habit has been formed a need has been created.

A glance at the *Radio Times* or *TV Times* reveals a pattern of programmes repeated week after week at exactly the same time. The effect is to make the viewer associate a particular programme with a particular time. Although it is not part of his job, his house or his family, a programme appearing regularly can seem an essential part of a man's life. To create and then fill this need in the viewing population a programme must not vary by much in its time or in its main characters.

Television tends to distrust the unfamiliar and to encourage repetition spiced with novelty. The effect is to present an audience with what look like new delights but never to make the newness so disturbing that a man is asked to think. The policy implies disrespect for the viewers by supposing that they are not open to new experiences.

Some of the wiser television bodies are aware of this situation and are prepared to spend money on programmes which break new ground even at the risk of attracting a smaller audience. In its early days *Z Cars* was one of these programmes.

From the start *Z Cars* concentrated on the work of the police rather than on the exploits of the criminals. Where the criminal and the law met, the interest was invariably on how the police dealt with a variety of situations. If the series had dramatized crime the effect would have been to make the criminal the hero and to leave to the police the repetitive and servile work of pursuit and capture. *Z Cars* tried to look not only at the criminal but also at the community through police eyes. In this way it showed what it was like to be a policeman and it investigated some of the complexities of law and order in a modern, urban society.

The policeman is often over-worked, with limited patience, limited sympathy and limited knowledge. He is picked out and isolated in a special uniform and confronted by a variety of disturbance, misfortune and extremity of behaviour. The old figure of a cheery, size twelve, paternal 'bobby' was appropriate to a village society but the modern city is very different. It is a place where rootless people take rooms, eye one another but keep to themselves, where the old can die of cold unnoticed, where a large number of offices and shops are deserted every night.

The best of the early *Z Cars* scripts tried to make the point that in these circumstances a new attitude to the law and the police is needed.

In answering the following questions you are asked **to use your own words** as far as possible, to keep within the required number of words, and *to use only information that is contained in the passage.*

a) What would appear to be the television companies' methods of attracting large audiences? (Use about **80** words.) [8]

b) In what ways were the early *Z Cars* programmes different from previous programmes involving the police? (**100** words should be sufficient.) [10]

c) According to the writer, what kind of needs can television best satisfy? (Answer in **two or three** sentences.)

Welsh Joint Education Committee, GCE, November, 1977.

4 *Read the following passages carefully and answer the questions which follow.*

Passage I

[George Orwell has been discussing boys' weekly papers and how they are basically unrealistic.]

The women's papers are aimed at an older public and are read for the most part by girls who are working for a living. Consequently they are on the surface much more realistic. It is taken for granted, for example, that nearly everyone has to live in a big
5   town and work at a more or less dull job. Sex, so far from being taboo, is *the* subject. The short, complete stories, the special feature of these papers, are generally of the romantic type: the heroine narrowly escapes losing her 'boy' to a designing rival, or the 'boy' loses his job and has to postpone marriage, but pres-
10   ently·gets a better job. The changeling-fantasy (a girl brought up in a poor home is 'really' the child of rich parents) is another favourite. Where sensationalism comes in, usually in the serials, it arises out of the more domestic type of crime, such as bigamy, forgery or sometimes murder; no Martians, death-rays or inter-
15   national anarchist gangs.

These papers are at any rate aiming at credibility, and they

have a link with real life in their correspondence columns, where
genuine problems are being discussed. Ruby M. Ayres's column of
advice in the *Oracle*, for instance, is extremely sensible and well
20 written. And yet the world of the *Oracle* and *Peg's Paper* is a pure
fantasy-world. It is the same fantasy all the time; pretending to be
richer than you are. The chief impression that one carries away
from almost every story in these papers is of a frightful, over-
whelming 'refinement'. Ostensibly the characters are working-
25 class people, but their habits, the interiors of their houses, their
clothes, their outlook and, above all, their speech are entirely
middle class. They are all living at several pounds a week above
their income. And needless to say, that is just the impression that
is intended. The idea is to give the bored factory-girl or worn-out
30 mother of five a dream-life in which she pictures herself – not
actually as a duchess but as, say, the wife of a bank-manager. Not
only is a five-to-six pound a week standard of life set up as an
ideal, it is tacitly assumed that that is how working-class people
really do live.
35   The major facts are simply not faced. It is admitted, for instance, that people sometimes lose their jobs; but then the dark
clouds roll away and they get better jobs instead. No mention of
unemployment as something permanent and inevitable, no mention of the dole, no mention of trade unionism. No suggestion
40 anywhere that there can be anything wrong with the system as a
system; there are only individual misfortunes, which are generally due to somebody's wickedness and can in any case be put
right in the last chapter. Always the dark clouds roll away, the
kind employer raises Alfred's wages, and there are jobs for every-
45 body except the drunks.

(Adapted from *Boys' Weeklies* by George Orwell)

Passage II

*[Passage I was written in 1939. Passage II was written about similar magazines
and stories in the 1950s.]*

The strongest impression, after one has read a lot of these
stories, is of their extraordinary fidelity to the detail of the
readers' lives. The short stories take up as much space as the
serial or long story, and they seem to be mainly faithful tran-
5   scripts of minor incidents, amusing or worrying, from ordinary
life. The serials may erupt into the startlingly posh world of what
are still called 'the stately homes of England', or present a Rajah
or a Sheik: but often the world is that the readers live in, with a
considerable accuracy in its particulars. A fair proportion of the
10 crime is of that world too – the distress when Mrs Thompson is
suspected of shoplifting, and so on.

A short story at the back of the *Oracle*, 'Hero's Homecoming',
opens: 'Most of the women who dealt at the little general store on
the corner of Roper's Road were rather tired of hearing about Mrs
15   Bolsom's boy, but they couldn't very well tell her so because she
was so obliging and so handy to run to at times of emergency.' A
typical *Lucky Star* one page story starts: 'Lilian West glanced at the
clock on the kitchen wall. "My goodness," she thought. "How
quickly I get through the housework these days!"' It goes on to
20   tell how, after deciding to leave her married children alone so as
not to be thought a nuisance, she found fresh happiness in
realizing how much she was still needed. 'Mary was an ordinary
girl doing an ordinary job in a factory,' another story begins, and
incidentally epitomizes the points of departure for almost all of
25   them.
　　Such a nearness to the detail of the lives of the readers might
be simply the prelude to an excursion into a wish-fulfilment story
about the surprising things that can happen to someone from that
world. Sometimes this is so, and there is occasionally a stepping-
30   up of the social level inside the stories, so that people can feel how
nice it would be to be a member of the Villa or good-class housing
groups. But often what happens is what might happen to anyone, and the environment is that of most readers.

(Adapted from *The Uses of Literacy* by Richard Hoggart)

Questions on Passage I:

1　Under a), b) and   c), state briefly the point Orwell is making in each of
the three paragraphs.   [12]

2　In Passage I Orwell claims that the stories in the women's papers are 'on
the surface much more realistic' than those in the boys' weeklies of the
period.

In not more than seventy words, set down clearly those elements referred
to in lines 1–34 of the passage that are intended to justify Orwell's claim.
                                                                          [12]

Question on Passage II:

3　In Passage II Richard Hoggart refers to 'the extraordinary fidelity to the
detail of the readers' lives' of the stories in the women's magazines.

What elements of their lives do the examples quoted by Hoggart illustrate? Write **about 100–150 words** of continuous prose.   [12]

Question on both passages:

4　Both writers refer to the idea of escape – Orwell speaks of 'fantasy'
Hoggart of 'wish-fulfilment'.

By summary, reference and quotation show how each writer uses the
idea of escape.   [12]

Oxford and Cambridge, Paper I, November, 1978.

5 *Write a summary of the following passage in good continuous prose, using not more than 120 words. State at the end of your summary the number of words you have used. The passage contains 346 words.* (16 marks)

After the legalisation of professionalism in soccer in 1885 the football following became too strong to be ignored. Such was the attraction that employers had to grant the "twelve o'clock Saturday" or face mass absenteeism. Not surprisingly it was in the hot-bed of soccer – north-east England's Tyne and Wearside – that engineering employers first conceded the Saturday half-holiday only five years afterwards. The fascination was still far from its climax. In the 1940s employers suffered again, this time from the magic of Stanley Matthews. It was accepted that his shuffling dribble should be allowed to shut the local works. A mid-week home match meant a mass exodus to see the "Wizard" no matter what official working hours might be.

Even at this time there was still something of the "cap-and-muffler" image about professional football. Many of the most skilled were indeed the products of back-street football, banding together to buy cheap balls to learn their juggling skills. The inducement was often the dream of earning enough money from football to buy a little shop that would take them away for ever from the grind of industry. Queen's Park, Glasgow's outstanding amateur club, commented acidly on the conversion of labourers into tobacconists.

Although there proved to be a greater pride and passion for the game among the working class, it was in the public schools and universities that the game first had proper organisation and following. The swing of the game from public-school preserve to public property was the outcome of the Cup, so often the catalyst in football's development. Blackburn's Cup team of 1883 was the first team to prepare for a match with a week's special training. The Cup Final was described in a newspaper report: "*Aristocrats versus artisans* would have suitably titled this memorable encounter between teams from the historic playing-fields of Eton and a nondescript eleven of working men from Blackburn. The Blackburn eleven, composed mainly of players of humble origin, gave such an exhibition as had never been seen before. Their tactics simply wore the Etonians off their legs."

AEB, Paper II, June 1978.

6 Oxford United Football Club are planning to move their ground to a new site in an area of Oxford called Marston.

Local residents disagree over whether or not this move should go ahead and the local paper has printed a selection of letters on the subject. Some of these letters are in favour of the move while some argue against it.

Read the letters carefully. Summarize the arguments made for and against the proposal and write a report of no more than 300 words in which you outline the various arguments made in the letters.

Why we say no

WE do not want any sports complex in this part of Oxford, particularly off the Northern Bypass which already has enough traffic on it. Any extra will only add to the congestion.

This area is in the green belt and in no circumstances should be built on, especially for something so unnecessary as a sports area and shopping precinct.

Miss L. Earle, 8 Woodfield Road.

ALISE United's present is not practical, but surely ving them from a shopping a to a large council estate d also a private estate is upid. I would have thought ne site proposed earlier further away from Marston was the better idea.

Most of those living on Boults Farm and Northway Estate have young families. Can we be assured we won't have soccer fans rampaging over the estate as they do in Headington?

I would also think the traffic problems in Marsh Lane and Headley Way would be horrendous; as it is the road is busy with traffic from and to the JR2.

As for only 100 out of 2,000 Marston residents not agreeing to the idea, I certainly have seen no such circular. I suggest Mr Bill Reeves checks his facts.

Carl A. Gunning, Northway Estate, Headington.

AS a resident (who incidentally did not receive a circular asking about the proposed move) I wholeheartedly disapprove of the plan.

Marston at present has a semi-rural character ideal for bringing up children and well provided for with an adventure playground, a cycle track and surrounding open fields.

The proposed development would turn the area between Marson and the ringroad into a tarmac wasteland which, on at least two occasions per week, would be noisy, strewn with litter and a totally unsuitable environment for young children.

If Oxford United must move from Headington then they should move outside the ring road where the noise and litter would find fewer people to offend and where the traffic would be less of a danger and an eyesore.

M. P. Williams, Buther's Close, Marston.

In the week that all 92 league chairmen met to discuss the supposed problems in the game, Mr Bill Reeves proudly announces yet another absurd scheme for rehousing lowly Oxford United.

With the club on the brink of a return to Fourth Division football and the Directors apparently ignorant of the shocking problems on the field, they persistently spend their energies in cahoots with a developer who is only using them as a stepping stone for a hypermarket permission.

This latest proposal has a ground capacity no larger than the Manor, no facilities for speedway, greyhound racing or athletics and it is difficult to see just what new benefits the development would provide that could not be created at the existing ground with a little perseverance and imagination.

We know that one of the topics discussed at the chairmen's meeting was violence on the terraces but surely United's directors are guilty of a very subtle form of hooliganism themselves which will lead to the financial ruin of the club and the loss of what little local support they still have.

What is so wrong with the Manor anyway Mr Reeves? It is a tidy little ground with facilities of a par with most second division clubs in an established position which may not be ideal but environmentally it is far preferable to the wholesale blitz of Marston's open spaces to provide a nasty 'plastic' motel and store complex, the likes of which can be seen around some of our Midlands cities.

An advert in this paper recently made it known that Oxford United are looking for extra directors – it failed to mention one qualification that apparently the present board do not possess – common sense!

I. J. Coleman, 9 Western Road, Kidlington.

Oxford Star November 13th–14th 1980

Why we say yes

I AM hopeful that United will get their new stadium. I am all for it; it will be good for Oxford, not just for football supporters but for the whole family.

With an all seated stadium I am sure it will cut out the hooliganism inside the ground; what happens outside the ground is a social problem.

I am pleading with the council to give the go-ahead because they can't build any more at the Manor. Let's have a super stadium we can be proud of.

M. A. Sumner, Iffley Road, Oxford.

I AM in favour of this marvellous idea.

I'm sure that the majority of the Oxford public would agree. The Manor must surely be one of the smallest grounds in the league.

Being all seated would cut the hooliganism down and husbands would at last be able to bring the whole family to watch the game, with no fear of fighting breaking out between supporters.

If the stadium is given the go-ahead the stands will be full.

Good luck!

Andrew Coleman (Loyal London Road Supporter), Oxford.

I AND my family – my wife and two daughters – are very much in favour of Oxford United's move to Marston.

We have followed the club for ten years or so, and will welcome the chance of an hour's shopping or badminton, a decent car park, which will accommodate visiting supporters' coaches and a seat in an up-to-date stadium. Let us give fans something they can be proud of.

We certainly have never been molested or troubled by hooliganism in any way but moronic behaviour is not confined to football crowds. What about the skinhead who threw a stone through my greenhouse out here in a remote village and the others who have pulled down my elderly neighbour's wall? Or those who did £10,000 worth of damage to new cars at Kidlington?

It will be much easier to police the crowds in a well-constructed stadium on a well-ordered site. I canvassed the Summertown area near the original site and to my surprise, the result, despite a lot of toffee-nosed people at Summer Fields and adjoining roads, split exactly 50–50.

Nearly everybody, whether in favour or not, agreed that Oxford was short of recreational facilities.

I hope that these facilities will not be unduly skimped. And the ratepayers don't pay a penny!

A. W. Milton, Abingdon.

Oxford Star November 13th–14th 1980

Letters

There are two different kinds of letter which you could be asked to write in the examination: the business letter, and the personal letter.

Business letters

This might be a letter of complaint, or a request for information, or an application for a job. It is written, in other words, to achieve a particular purpose, and what is therefore important is that it is clear, concise, and set out in the correct way.

Here is an example of a business letter:

```
                                        28  Caledonia Close
                                        Oxford  OX2 72X

The Manager
Sherborne Electrical Goods
Berkeley Place
Oxford  OX7 35J                         30th November, 1981

Dear Sir,

        I bought a Supremo washing machine in your shop on September 13th
this year.  The machine is, therefore, still under guarantee. This morning
it developed a leak and flooded the kitchen.  I clearly cannot use the
machine until this fault is rectified, and would be grateful if an engineer
could call at the earliest opportunity.  I am at home every afternoon
between two and five, and my telephone number is Oxford 3234.

Yours faithfully,

D. James .

D. James
```

Since this is a formal letter, it is normal to write the address of the person to whom you are sending the letter at the top left hand side of the page. It is also normal to start the letter 'Dear Sir' and to finish it 'Yours faithfully'.

The tone of the letter is formal. No effort has been made to be friendly and chatty: the aim is simply to state the necessary information in as concise and clear a way as possible.

☐ Now write the following letters. Set out each letter in the correct way.

a) To a local garage asking to arrange a test drive in their latest model.

b) To a travel agent complaining that your hotel did not meet the standards which you expected.

c) To a local employer asking whether they have any job vacancies, and giving a brief description of yourself and of your qualifications.

Personal letters

A business letter is written to someone you do not know. It is written in order to make a specific point and every word in the letter should be relevant to the end which you wish to achieve. A personal letter, on the other hand, is the sort of letter which you might write to a friend or a relative. It can be much less formal in tone, and much fuller in its descriptive and personal detail. Quite what you write in a personal letter will obviously depend on the circumstances in which you are writing, but it is worth remembering that there is no real difference between the skills needed to write an interesting, stimulating letter and those needed to write an evocative description or a realistic characterization. Your aim in writing a personal letter ought, in other words, to be to involve the reader in what it is you are describing, and you will do this if you can select vivid and memorable details and organize these details to maximum effect.

This is clearly an example of a question which demands a personal letter.

You have quarrelled with your friend and now feel that you were largely to blame. Write a letter which you hope will restore the friendship. (Supply the appropriate layout).

Welsh Joint Education Committee O Level 7.11.77

A possible answer to the question might run as follows.

> 28 Caledonia Close
> Oxford OX2 72X
> 1st September 1981

Dear Jane,

  I've been thinking a lot about what happened on holiday and I'm writing to say that I'm sorry. I didn't realise that you minded quite so much about Gary and me going to the cinema. If I had understood your feelings I would not have gone with him.

  The photos I took have just come back from the printers, and some of them came out really well. Do you remember when that farmer chased us off his land, and I took a picture of him as he stood there shaking his stick at us and looking as if he was about to have a fit? Well, that is one of the best. It makes me laugh every time I look at it! There are some good ones of the beach, too, particularly of that day when the sea was really rough and the waves were smashing in on us so fiercely. You look freezing in one picture, standing in about two inches of water, covered in goose pimples and trembling quietly to yourself! That was the time when Richard threw you in, wasn't it?

  Anyway it was a very enjoyable holiday. I just hope you agree with me, and that you don't still feel angry. Why don't you ring me up? There's a party at the Club next week and we could go together.

> Love,
> Amanda

The problem with writing a 'personal' letter in an examination is, of course, that it cannot really be personal, and this is perhaps obvious in the above example. The difference between a personal and a business letter should, however, now be clear.

☐ Remembering that the tone of any personal letter depends very much on your relationship with the person to whom you are writing, write the following letters. Set each letter out in the correct way.

To a relative thanking her for your Christmas present, and telling her what you did over the holiday.

To a very close friend who now goes to a school in a different part of the country, telling her/him all the latest gossip.

To someone you met at a dance and would like to see again.

Communicating information

☐ Read the following newspaper report on the way in which smoking has increased in the developing countries.

THE DECLINE in smoking in Europe and North America has been matched by a dramatic increase in the developing countries, according to the World Health Organisation.

In a review of its 1980 campaign, 'Smoking or Health – the Choice is Yours,' the WHO said that smoking in developing countries is increasing due to the 'emulation of life-styles practised in industrial countries deliberately promoted by tobacco companies.'

Smoking-related diseases are increasing as a result, said the review.

The world tobacco market is dominated by seven companies, including British American Tobacco, Imperial and Rothmans. Between them the seven companies spend around £1,000 million a year on advertising. Faced with tougher controls on advertising in Western countries, the companies are turning to the Third World where controls are more lax.

People in developing countries are, it seems, being persuaded by advertising that affluent people normally smoke, though non-smokers outnumber smokers in Britain, the United States, Sweden and other Western countries.

In the United States, 30 million smokers have successfully kicked the habit since 1964 and only one in three Americans now smoke.

Most Western countries have strict controls over tobacco advertising, but in some Third World countries the promotion of tobacco appears to be virtually out of control.

The WHO said that in Malaysia more money is spent on tobacco promotion than on any other advertising, accounting for 9 per cent of the advertising bill. Malaysians over the age of 15 smoke an average of 2,000 cigarettes a year.

The tobacco industry in Nigeria has launched a 'massive marketing campaign,' the WHO said.

Cigarettes can generally be sold in the Third World without health warnings on the packets, although Sri Lanka has made these obligatory.

The Kenya Government has banned smoking in public places including transport and cinemas, to try to curb smoking-related diseases.

There is evidence that some of the tobacco companies are selling stronger, and thus more addictive, cigarettes in developing countries than they do in the West.

Tests at laboratories in Tennessee found that the State Express 555 cigarettes – a British American Tobacco product – contained 18 mg of tar when marketed in Britain but 31 mg of tar when sold in Kenya. The nicotine content was 0.9 per cent mg when sold in in Britain but 2 per cent mg when sold in Kenya.

The company's latest annual report spoke of 'considerable growth' in tobacco sales and profits in Asia, expansion of cigarette manufacturing in Brazil and Argentina and 'significant increases' in profits in El Salvador and Honduras.

The *British Medical Journal* said in a recent leading article that the British Government bears a special responsibility for the conduct of the tobacco industry in developing countries, 'because this country is the base for some of the world's largest multi-national tobacco companies.'

Observer 4.1.81

There are three points worth making about the way in which this report is written.

Firstly, it is extremely clear. The facts follow logically one after the other so that there is little chance that anyone reading it will become lost.

Secondly, everything included in the report is relevant to the central subject matter. This might seem an obvious enough point to make, but when you yourself attempt this kind of writing you will realize that it is by no means easy to decide what should be included in your report and what left out.

Thirdly, although, for the sake of clarity, the sentences tend to be short, the passage as a whole reads quite smoothly.

☐ Bear each of these points in mind when you are writing an essay in which you are trying to tell your reader something or explain something to him.

☐ Now attempt the following three questions. Each question is taken from an actual examination paper and involves the writing of some kind of report.

1 Hareton, a town of 4,720 inhabitants, is situated in North-West England, 20 miles south of Scotland. Here are some facts about the town:

its main source of employment, a factory which manufactures paper goods, has a number of vacancies in all departments;

education is its second highest employer of labour;

the number of Hareton's inhabitants is gradually decreasing;

its main recreational facilities are: 11 Public Houses; Football Club (2 teams); Cricket Club (3 teams); Ladies' Hockey Club (2 teams); Rugby Club (3 teams); Theatre Club (3 plays a year); Young Farmers' Club (55 members); Motor Club (150 members); Cubs (31 members); Brownies (37 members).

Imagine that you are *one* of the following:

i) A 16 year-old school-leaver with three O-level qualifications who wants an office job and who enjoys attending discos and professional football matches.

ii) The father of three young children, at present working in a large factory in the North of England.

iii) A University graduate who wants a job which will allow him/her time for sporting and cultural interests.

iv) A widow, with two teenage children, who has worked in a cotton-mill in recent years.

Having read the facts about Hareton, write about a page explaining your reasons for **either** wanting **or** not wanting to live and work there. You may wish to use the information given to support your answer.

JMB   GCE English Language Ordinary Alternative B 6.6.78

2 You are a reporter for the local newspaper.
The phone on your desk rings and when you answer it you hear your
Editor telling you to go and report on an explosion in the High Street.
You pick up your notebook and go.
The time is 10.20 am.

When you get back the Editor tells you to write your article as quickly as
possible since he is holding space on the front page. He needs the
headline immediately and this is what you choose –

BLAST WRECKS TOWN STORE

The relevant two pages of your notebook are reproduced below. Use the
information to write your article.

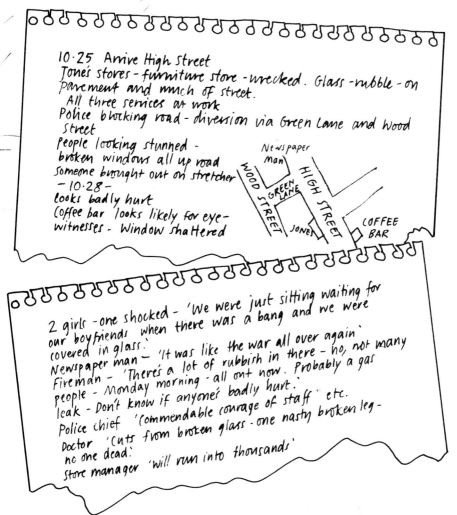

West Midlands Examinations Board   CSE English Studies Paper II

June 1978

3 A group of pupils from your school intends to visit the Royal Pennine Show and you have been asked to arrange the visit.

Study the programme below and the plan on the opposite page.

Write a report indicating the special attractions of the show for the group concerned. Include in it suggestions about possible meeting places and a time-table for the visit so that you might cater for different interests.

ROYAL PENNINE SHOW

PROGRAMME

GRAND RING EVENTS

12.00	Band of Grenadier Guards
1.00	Parade of New Agricultural Machinery
2.00	Show Jumping
3.15	Presentation of Show Jumping awards by the Queen Mother
3.45	Hevisi War Drums and Dancers from Ceylon
4.30	Fox-hound Parade
5.00	Red Devils Parachute Jump
5.30	Band of Grenadier Guards

All other Judging Events outside Grand Ring start at 3.45 and are expected to last an hour.

Entrance Charge to Ground – £1.00; Students – 50p;
Grand Ring – 50p

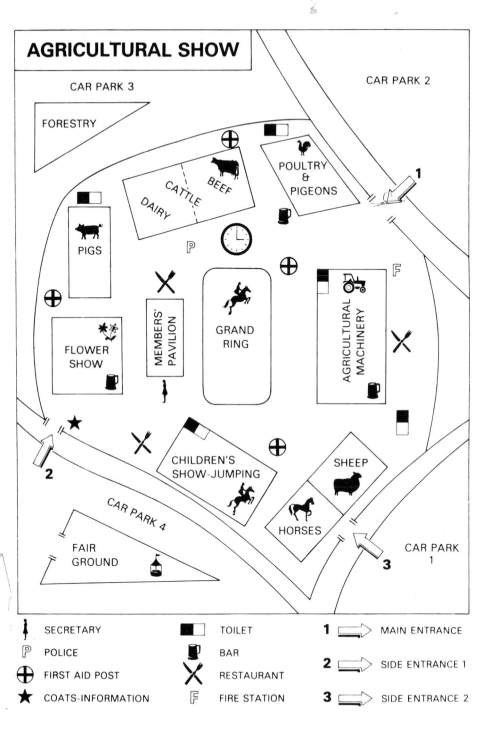

AGRICULTURAL SHOW

CAR PARK 3

CAR PARK 2

FORESTRY

CATTLE

DAIRY

BEEF

POULTRY & PIGEONS

1

PIGS

P

FLOWER SHOW

MEMBERS' PAVILION

GRAND RING

AGRICULTURAL MACHINERY

F

CHILDREN'S SHOW-JUMPING

SHEEP

2

HORSES

CAR PARK 4

FAIR GROUND

3

CAR PARK 1

SECRETARY		TOILET		**1**	MAIN ENTRANCE
POLICE		BAR		**2**	SIDE ENTRANCE 1
FIRST AID POST		RESTAURANT		**3**	SIDE ENTRANCE 2
COATS-INFORMATION		FIRE STATION			

Associated Lancashire Schools Examining Board
Joint Matriculation Board
Yorkshire Regional Examinations Board

Joint 16+ 1978

Writing explanations

A good explanation of how to do something or of how something works, like the good report, should be *clear, to the point* and *fluently written*.

☐ Read, as an example of how a potentially confusing procedure can be explained clearly, this account from a photography manual of how to set up a dark room. As you read, try and decide what it is about this explanation which makes it easy to follow.

Setting up a darkroom at home
A spare room fitted with purpose-built work benches and shelves and permanently blacked out is the ideal starting point for good darkroom procedure. Here your equipment can remain undisturbed between processing sessions. For many, though, a more makeshift arrangement is necessary, making temporary use of a bathroom or kitchen. Surfaces and materials may have to be removed at the end of each session, and equipment that can be stored easily is therefore an advantage.

The essential requirements
To be suitable as a darkroom, a room must fulfil three essential requirements. Firstly, it must be able to be easily and effectively blacked out. Even a small amount of light creeping around the door frame could be enough to spoil unprocessed film and paper. Secondly, mains electricity is needed to power the enlarger and safelight. A permanent darkroom may also need power to run other items, such as print dryer or light box. Ventilation to clear fumes from processing chemicals is the third requirement if many hours of work are anticipated, as lightproofing can block the free flow of air.

A factor that is convenient but not essential is a supply of running water so that films and prints can be washed and chemicals mixed without leaving the room. If this is not possible, films and prints can be placed in a bucket of water after processing and washed later.

The dry area
Whether permanent or temporary, your darkroom should be divided into two distinct areas of activity. A dry area should be reserved for all activities that do not involve the use of water or chemicals, such as selecting negatives or exposing paper in the enlarger or contact printer. The dry bench must be firm so that the enlarger does not vibrate during exposure. You should group near the enlarger a print easel, a seconds timer for timing exposures, dodgers and burners; negative files, printing papers, scissors and scalpel. An added help is a focus magnifier (to examine the image under the enlarger) and a print trimmer.

A print dryer should be separated from both the dry and wet areas, as you are handling wet prints, they must be kept away from negatives and other materials. At the same time, the dryer itself should be protected from chemical contamination.

The wet area
In this area of your darkroom chemicals are mixed and processed. Black and white processing involves three steps: developing the latent image, stopping the action of the developer and fixing the image (making the paper insensitive to further exposure to white light). The three dishes necessary for this process should be arranged so that the fixer dish (for the last step) is next to the sink. The safelight should be positioned above the developer dish.

John Hedgecoe's Introductory Photography Course 1979

The secret of a successful explanation is a firm grasp of whatever it is that you are writing about. To help you sort out your own thinking, it is often helpful to list everything which is involved in the description in note form before you start writing. If you do this, you can often spot which is the clearest and most logical way to write the explanation.

☐ Bearing this advice in mind, write clear explanations of how to do *two* of the following activities.

      a) load a camera with film
      b) wire a plug
      c) tie a shoe lace
      d) repair a puncture
      e) cook one of your favourite meals

Commenting on statistics

You may be faced in the examination by a question which asks you to comment on a timetable or table of statistics. Essentially, this kind of question calls for exactly the same skills which have been stressed in the previous two sections of this chapter: your commentary or report should be clear, to the point, and fluent.

The question which follows on the next page is a fairly representative example of what you might be asked to do.

In tackling a question like this it is essential that you work out exactly what you intend to say *before* you start writing.

For example, the first point to note as you study this timetable is that one disadvantage of the new timetable is that you will have to spend an hour in Leyburn whereas previously you could travel straight through.

Go through the timetable making two lists: one of the advantages, the other of the disadvantages. Then write your commentary, organizing it into two parts: the first dealing with the advantages, the second with the disadvantages.

You live in Hawes and need to travel by bus on three days a week. On Tuesdays and Thursdays you travel to Richmond and back. On Fridays you travel to Darlington and back. The times given in the old time-table have suited you well. Compare the two time-tables and explain the advantages and disadvantages for you of each.

	OLD TIMES		NEW TIMES	
	(outward journey)		(outward journey)	
	Tue. Thurs.	Fri.	Tue. Thurs.	Fri.
HAWES	7.50	10.00	7.50	7.50
Leyburn	8.51	11.08	8.51 (arr.) 9.51 (dep.)	8.51 (arr.) 9.51 (dep.)
Richmond	9.00	12.07 (arr.) 12.15 (dep.)	10.00	10.00 (arr.) 12.30 (dep.)
Darlington	—	12.45	—	13.00
	(return journey)		(return journey)	
Darlington	—	17.00	—	13.30
Richmond	17.45	17.30 (arr.) 17.45 (dep.)	17.45	14.00 (arr.) 17.45 (dep.)
Leyburn	18.22	18.22	18.22 (arr.) 19.52 (dep.)	18.22
HAWES	19.28	19.28	20.58	19.28

Associated Lancashire Schools Examining Board CSE (Alternative A) May 1978

Now try and answer the next two questions.

1 In January 1980 *The Times* newspaper published the results of a survey conducted by the Opinion Research Centre into what people think about trade unions.

The answers which people gave to two of the questions which they were asked in this survey are printed below in statistical form. Study these answers carefully and write a report in which you summarize the findings in continuous prose.

Question   Some people feel that British trade unions have too much power and show too little responsibility. Do you think this is true or not?

	All	Non trade union workers	Trade union members	Active trade union members
True	78	83	68	56
Untrue	16	11	27	39
Don't know	6	6	5	5

Question   Which of these statements is closest to your own opinion?

	All	Con	Lab	Lib	Others
Strikers' families should get social security benefits from the State	19	5	34	13	20
Strikers' families should only get social security benefits when union funds are exhausted	27	28	24	32	24
Strikers' families should not get social security benefits	19	26	12	19	19
Strikers' families should get social security benefits – but the money should be paid back when the strike is over	31	37	26	34	28
None of these	2	3	0	1	4
Don't know	2	1	4	1	4

The Times 21.1.80

2 The following tables are taken from a national survey of our attitudes towards disabled people. Study each table carefully, and write a report in continous prose summarizing the findings.

On which way of helping severely handicapped old people should the authorities spend most money?

	all respondents	people who know a disabled person	
		in own family	other family
	%	%	%
provide better facilities at home	35	39	37
more residential centres	34	35	34
both equally	25	21	24
don't know	6	4	5

Attitudes to the disabled

	all respondents		all knowing a disabled person	
	agree	disagree	agree	disagree
	%	%	%	%
the disabled should be expected to bear their share of the country's sacrifices	35	46	36	46
physically disabled children should, as far as possible, go to ordinary schools	71	22	75	20
mentally handicapped children should, as far as possible, go to ordinary schools	35	55	37	54
more women should be prepared to stay at home to care for disabled relations	44	33	45	33
male respondents to last question	48	30	—	—
female respondents	41	35	—	—

If your son, daughter or close friend, said they were going to marry a disabled person, would it be a good or bad idea if the person were:

	all respondents		all knowing a disabled person	
	'good idea'	'bad idea'	'good idea'	'bad idea'
	%	%	%	%
physically handicapped by loss of a limb	46	19	52	16
mentally ill	8	68	8	69
blind	49	20	55	16
deaf	54	15	60	12
mentally handicapped	8	64	10	64

New Society 1.1.81

Chapter Five

Argument

Passages which present an argument are sometimes set as comprehension exercises in the examination. Most boards also include a question which involves the candidate in developing his or her own argument as part of the essay section of the examination. It is therefore important in preparing for the examination that you can both understand and criticize someone else's argument and write a persuasive essay of your own. This chapter helps you to develop each of these skills.

In everyday life it is similarly important that you can evaluate arguments which are put to you. Pick up a newspaper or turn on the television and the chances are that someone will be trying to persuade you that their particular point of view is the correct one. Should marijuana be legalized? Should the abortion laws be tightened? Should the police be armed? These are just three controversial issues which are often debated publically. If you are to come to an intelligent personal decision about such issues, you must be able to criticize the case which is put to you.*

Techniques of persuasion

There are basically three tactics which writers use in order to persuade their readers to accept their point of view. The three passages which follow illustrate these tactics. Read each passage carefully and answer the questions which are set on it.

SLADDEN WOOD, near Dover, was once a popular local beauty spot. Sixteen acres of ash and maple, a home for nightingales and rare orchids. Three years ago, bulldozers moved in and flattened it.

Five years ago, Ashton Keynes Long Meadow in Wiltshire was one of the last haunts of the snakeshead fritillary. This exotic-looking flower is now so rare that it is more or less confined to 15 fields in nine counties, but it thrived on this particular 11-acre site until 1975. Then the meadow changed hands. The new owner "improved" his land and the fritillaries are gone.

Incidents like these seldom make headlines. Although both localities had been officially designated by the Nature Conservancy Council as "Sites of Special Scientific Interest," their loss passed almost without comment. But they are typical examples of the piecemeal destruction which is rapidly depriving Britain of its remaining wildlife habitats.

Brian Jackman *The Sunday Times* 14.12.80

*For further help on this topic, see Part B, Chapter One, pages 162–166

1 What was special about Sladden Wood?

2 What was special about Ashton Keynes Long Meadow?

3 What happened to each of these important places?

4 What exactly is the point Brian Jackman is making?

What Brian Jackman does in this passage is base his argument very firmly on the evidence which he quotes. He hopes to convince you that conservation is an important issue by citing two examples of places where commercial interests have triumphed over ecological concern.

This is a clear example of an argument which depends for its effect on the evidence which the writer cites. In planning an essay of your own on a controversial topic, you should certainly consider whether you have any evidence of this factual kind which you can include to support your case.

> Man has come to dominate the earth and to prosper by his cleverness. With the tools and technological knowledge now at his command, he not only tinkers with his environment to make it more comfortable – he rapes it. We continue, nevertheless, to use brute force to make natural resources yield up what we want – now – from them. Danger signals blink urgently on all sides. Our survival really is in the balance.
>
> Rachel Carson *Silent Spring* 1963

1 Summarize in one sentence the argument which is being made here.

2 Is there *any* evidence of the kind which Brian Jackman cites in this passage?

3 What is the force of the verbs 'tinker' and 'rape'?

4 Why does the writer enclose the word 'now' in dashes?

5 What is the effect of the two short, crisp sentences which end the passage?

Rachel Carson's argument here does not depend on precise evidence. She chooses rather to persuade her readers through the force of her language. The words she uses and the actual structure of her sentences – their shortness and abruptness – communicate to the reader her sense of the dangers which mankind faces. Again, this is a tactic which you would do well to consider in relation to your own writing.

> The train bore me away, through the monstrous scenery of slag-heaps, chimneys, piled scrap-iron, foul canals, paths of cindery mud criss-crossed by the prints of clogs. This was March, but the weather had been horribly cold and everywhere there were mounds of blackened snow. As we moved slowly through the outskirts of the town we passed row after row of little grey slum houses running at right angles to the embankment. At the back of one of the houses a young woman was kneeling on the stones, poking a stick up the leaden waste-pipe which ran from

the sink inside and which I suppose was blocked. I had time to see everything about her – her sacking apron, her clumsy clogs, her arms reddened by the cold. She looked up as the train passed, and I was almost near enough to catch her eye. She had a round pale face, the usual exhausted face of the slum girl who is twenty-five and looks forty, thanks to miscarriages and drudgery; and it wore, for the second in which I saw it, the most desolate, hopeless expression I have ever seen. It struck me then that we are mistaken when we say that 'It isn't the same for them as it would be for us,' and that people bred in the slums can imagine nothing but the slums. For what I saw in her face was not the ignorant suffering of an animal. She knew well enough what was happening to her – understood as well as I did how dreadful a destiny it was to be kneeling there in the bitter cold, on the slimy stones of a slum backyard, poking a stick up a foul drain-pipe.

George Orwell   *The Road to Wigan Pier* 1937

1 What sort of landscape is described in the first three sentences?
2 Why does George Orwell set the scene in this way before introducing the young woman?
3 In your own words describe this woman's appearance.
4 This is not an argument for a specific course of action but there is no doubt that Orwell wants his readers to react in a particular way to what he describes. What reaction do you think he wants to inspire?

The tactic here is neither to quote precise evidence nor to state the argument in a forceful and persuasive fashion. It is rather to approach the subject in a less direct and more personal way. What Orwell does is involve the reader in the young woman's life through his detailed and imaginative description. He leaves the details to speak for themselves and the reader to draw his or her own conclusions.

Your own writing

Either: The world would have been a much better place without the motor car.

Or: The unions have become too powerful.

☐ Go to the library and find out something about one of these two subjects. Make up your mind what your opinion is on the subject you have chosen. Write a paragraph of no more than 150 words to persuade people that your opinion is correct. Base your argument in the evidence you have found.

Either: Marriage is an out-dated and unnecessary institution.

Or: Every pregnant woman has the right to an abortion. It is up to her, and her alone.

☐ Choose one of these controversial statements. Decide what your point of view is on the issue you have chosen. Write a paragraph of no more than 150 words in which you persuade people to accept this point of view through the force of your language.

Either: Christmas today is no more than an excuse for a commercial binge.

Or: Since few people go to church, it is absurd that RE should remain a compulsory subject in schools.

☐ Choose one of these titles. Again, decide what your own opinion is. Think about a particular Christmas or an RE lesson which you have experienced. Describe this experience in such a way that your description persuades people that your opinion is correct. Use no more than 150 words.

Constructing an argument

The passages in the first part of this chapter were chosen because they exemplified one particular tactic or strategy which writers can use to persuade their readers. Most arguments, however, make use of more than one such tactic, and the passages which you will now read are more typical of the arguments which you meet in everyday life in that their writers use more than one strategy to persuade you to accept their point of view.

☐ The questions which follow each passage are designed to make you think both about how the argument is constructed and about the actual issues which are raised.

One laudable aim from all points of view would be to ensure that only wanted children were born. While it is undoubtedly true that unwanted children later become accepted and loved, it is also true that the casebook of the NSPCC is full of tragic
5 examples of the unwanted and unloved.
Caspar Brook, director of the Family Planning Association, reckons that there are 200–300,000 unwanted pregnancies each year. Though more and more children are being deliberately conceived out of wedlock, the signs are that a high proportion of
10 the 150,000 unmarried women who become pregnant each year do not want their babies – some have put the figure as high as 100,000. Mrs Helene Graham, assistant director of the Family Planning Association, has stated that around three million women of child-bearing age in Britain do not practise birth con-
15 trol, mainly through ignorance.
A really comprehensive education programme in the schools should have top priority in any population policy. It is not only a

matter of giving sex instruction, but of encouraging responsible attitudes and making sure that the consequences of irresponsible
20 behaviour are appreciated. A programme of this kind could not only result in fewer unwanted children being born, but less distress for young girls and their families, lower social costs when children have to be taken into care and so on. Ignorance on this subject is still profound. It should not be assumed that because
25 sex is more freely discussed these days, all young people are aware of the facts of life. *Daily Mirror* columnist Marjorie Proops told a Royal Society of Health conference that teenagers still believed old wives' tales about sex. Girls of 14 and over thought that holding their breath during intercourse was a protection
30 against pregnancy and others thought that standing up meant they would not conceive. A survey carried out by Hertfordshire County Council revealed that one in five girls aged 14 believed that only women could use contraceptives.

What young people are getting is a super-abundance of titil-
35 lation and commercialized eroticism and all too little genuine instruction.

Those backwoodsmen – and women – who thunder on about sin and retribution might bear in mind that the result in many cases is that an unwanted child becomes yet another
40 burden for the local authority to bear, paid for by you and I.

To support the educational drive, birth-control facilities should be freely available in the schools, universities, through the National Health Service and so on. This is not, as some would have it, licensing promiscuity but recognizing a situation that
45 exists and trying to do something about it.

H. F. Wallis   *The New Battle of Britain* 1972

1 One characteristic of the convincing argument is that the writer has foreseen possible objections to his case. This is true of this passage. In the first and last paragraphs, for instance, the writer forestalls two possible criticisms which his readers might make. What are these criticisms?

2 To some extent this is an argument which depends on the evidence which is quoted.

    – What are the figures quoted in paragraph two intended to prove?

    – Why does the writer quote Marjorie Proops' comments in paragraph three?

    – It is always important in reading an argument to think about the nature of the evidence cited. Do you think that these stories which Marjorie Proops tells should carry as much weight as the figures quoted in paragraph two? Give reasons for your answer.

3 The impact of paragraphs four and five lies not in any evidence which is quoted but in the forcefulness of the writer's language.

– Explain in your own words the phrase 'a super-abundance of titillation and commercialized eroticism.' (lines 34–5)

– What does the writer hope to achieve through his use of the noun 'backwoodsmen' and verb 'thunder'? (line 37)

– Is it fair of him to use these words?

4 Write a short essay (200–300 words) in reply to this argument, stating whether you agree or disagree with the case put forward and giving reasons for your reaction.

From 'The Sporting Spirit'

I am always amazed when I hear people saying that sport creates goodwill between the nations, and that if only the common peoples of the world could meet one another at football or cricket, they would have no inclination to meet on the battle-
5   field . . .
Nearly all the sports practised nowadays are competitive. You play to win, and the game has little meaning unless you do your utmost to win. On the village green, where you pick up sides and no feeling of local patriotism is involved, it is possible to play
10 simply for the fun and exercise: but as soon as the question of prestige arises, as soon as you feel that you and some larger unit will be disgraced if you lose, the most savage combative instincts are aroused. Anyone who has played even in a school football match knows this. At the international level sport is frankly
15 mimic warfare. But the significant thing is not the behaviour of the players but the attitude of the spectators, of the nations who work themselves into furies over these absurd contests, and seriously believe – at any rate for short periods – that running, jumping and kicking a ball are tests of national virtue.
20 As soon as strong feelings of rivalry are aroused, the notion of playing the game according to the rules always vanishes. People want to see one side on top and the other side humiliated, and they forget that victory gained through cheating or through the intervention of the crowd is meaningless. Even when the spec-
25 tators don't intervene physically they try to influence the game by cheering their own side and "rattling" opposing players with boos and insults. Serious sport has nothing to do with fair play. It is bound up with hatred, jealousy, boastfulness, disregard of all rules and sadistic pleasure in witnessing violence: in other words
30 it is war minus the shooting.

George Orwell   (in *Shooting an Elephant*)   1950

1 Using your own words summarize in one sentence the argument which George Orwell is making here.

2 What is it, according to Orwell, that turns a game played simply for pleasure into something much more serious and violent?

3 Explain the phrase 'mimic warfare'.

4 How, in Orwell's view, do spectators of international sport behave?

5 Is any evidence quoted here, or are all these statements Orwell's personal opinions?

6 This argument depends for its effect on the dramatic way in which Orwell writes.

Which sentence seems to you to be the most forceful and dramatic?

Do you think that the statements are exaggerated to the point where they weaken rather than strengthen the argument?

7 Write a reply to Orwell in which you defend international sport. Answer Orwell's arguments and include any points in favour of international competition which might strengthen your case.

Only about one-third of Britain's 2,700 miles of coastline are now worth fighting for, according to the National Trust. The rest is deemed to be too sick to recover, having been desecrated by various kinds of development, inundated with caravans, shacks
5 and shanties or barred to the public by the Services. The Englishman's ration of coast amounts, in fact, to no more than four inches.

With two-thirds of us still having to take our holidays in July and August, it is hardly surprising, therefore, that the popular
10 resorts, especially those in the West Country, are deluged with cars and people, that peace and quiet is at a premium and that recreational resources are overstrained, with speedboats interfering with anglers and swimmers, water ski-iers with surfers, and sand yachters with those who just want to build sandcastles
15 or sit on the beach. And there are likely to be 20 million more people taking holidays at home in ten years' time, making 50 million in all.

Cars are such a problem in the smaller resorts that one or two have stopped them from entering the town centre, and more will
20 probably have to follow suit. Some measure of the problem is contained in the fact that on a fine summer's day 2½ miles of front at Barry, in Glamorgan, has to accommodate 10,000 cars! And it is forecast that there will be twice as many cars on the road by 1980.
25 If only we had had the foresight to stop so much coastal development taking place! This has either barred the public from the foreshore or made it so unattractive that nobody would choose to go there. The proportion of built-up area along the coast is, in fact, twice as great as for the country as a whole. On
30 the other hand, it may not be generally realised that there is no general right for the public to use the beaches. These are mostly owned by the Crown, but some are in the hands of local authorities and private individuals. People are only permitted to

bathe, sunbathe and build sandcastles by the forbearance of the
35 owners; except for sea fishermen, who have been granted a right
under Magna Carta to fish from the shore, a right they share only
with those engaged in navigation.

However, the harm which has been done to the two-thirds
makes it all the more essential to preserve what remains. About
40 10 per cent lies within the area of our ten national parks and is
thereby subject to development restrictions. Nearly a quarter
(about 900 miles) have been designated as areas of outstanding
natural beauty, which means that they are protected, though less
stringently. The National Trust and Nature Conservancy own
45 much beautiful coastal land, and the Trust will doubtless be
adding to its acquisitions considerably as a result of the funds
received from 'Enterprise Neptune'.

Development should as far as possible be confined to areas
already built up, and even here should be strictly controlled. The
50 borough of Crosby, in Lancashire, has shown the way. Faced
with plans by Mersey Docks and Harbour Board to extend the
dock system further north, which it was felt would ruin the
foreshore and seafront and cause pollution, the borough council
at first opposed the project and, when this failed, made a con-
55 dition that proper landscaping be carried out. Under the agreed
scheme, the council is constructing a sea wall and enclosing 166
acres of the shore, 100 of which will be grassed and the remainder
turned into a boating lake. The project (estimated cost £400,000)
received an award in the conservation awards scheme for 1971
60 sponsored jointly by *The Times* and the Royal Institution of
Chartered Surveyors, and the judges commended the council on
its 'vision and imagination'.

All kinds of studies have been made or are in progress – by
the Nature Conservancy, British Tourism Authority and the
65 Countryside Commission. In its publication, *The Planning of the
Coastline*, the commission recommends that regional coastal
parks be created and that the coast should be cleared of disfigure-
ment caused by derelict military structures or other unsightly
works, and argues strongly that special attention must be given
70 to those coasts where the scenery is judged to be equal in merit to
that found in national parks. This argument is amplified in a
separate document, *The Coastal Heritage*, in which 34 areas are
recommended for designation as Heritage Coasts.

Many studies of future needs and how they might be met are
75 being carried out by planning authorities. All this concern,
though belated, is welcome, but it should not stop there. Any
progress in this respect will be nullified unless we can stop the
seas themselves becoming polluted by oil, untreated sewage and
the huge quantities of industrial waste and other junk now being
80 dumped in it. Primitive practices like the dumping of three
million tons of spoil a year into the sea from the collieries near
Blackhall in Co. Durham, which makes miles of coastline un-

usable, represents a criminal disregard for amenity which should not be tolerated.

H. F. Wallis   *The New Battle of Britain* 1972

1 Britain's coastline has been spoilt in three ways. What are these ways?
2 What is the meaning of the words 'desecrated' (line 3 and 'deluged' (line 10)?

   Explain why the writer has chosen to use these particular verbs.
3 What problem is discussed in the second paragraph?
4 There are two reasons why much coastal development should have been prevented (lines 26–8). What are these reasons?
5 Explain *in one sentence* what action the borough of Crosby took against plans to develop the dock system to the north of the town.
6 What three recommendations were made in the Countryside Commission's publication *The Planning of the Coastline* (lines 65–71)?
7 Summarize the argument made in this passage *in one sentence*.
8 Do you find this argument persuasive or not? Give reasons for your answer.
9 The writer of this passage has not chosen to describe a particular stretch of coastline which has been spoilt. Such a description could, however, be an effective way of persuading people to take an interest in this issue. Write such a description. Use around 250 words and try to create as detailed and convincing a picture as you can. Anybody who has read your description should be able to feel what a ruined stretch of coastline is actually like.

Evaluating an argument

As a final test of your ability to evaluate arguments and come to an independent personal decision, read the following comments on the controversial question of whether Britain should allow heavy articulated lorries to use our roads.

In 1980 Sir Arthur Armitage led an inquiry into this issue. The week before his report was published *The Sunday Times* printed two articles about the impact which heavy lorries can have on the environment.

Read these articles. Write a short summary of the argument made in each article.

Monsters of Mayfield

ACCORDING to the guide-books, Mayfield is an ancient Wealden village where St Dunstan fought off the devil in the tenth century. According to the villagers, locked in the battle with their 20th-century fiend, the juggernaut, Mayfield is a village of insomniacs and St Dunstan had it easy.

Mayfield is a "pinch point" on the A267 nine miles south of Tunbridge Wells. Its high street shrinks to 19ft wide at one point and in two places there are no pavements. People are afraid to use their front doors. Shopkeepers yell at their customers to make themselves heard and ped-estrians cringe along the pavements. Mayfield is one of many hundreds of British villages battered by the passage of heavy lorries. It sent evidence to Sir Arthur Armitage's inquiry about what life is like there since the A267 was "discovered" by lorry drivers on their way to and from Newhaven: how one woman was hit by a lorry wing-mirror and permanently disabled; how people cannot sleep at night or converse by day; how vibration has shattered glasses and chipped tiles; how tourists have stopped coming.

It would now like to add to its catalogue of ills: eight gas leaks have been found in the high street in the past fort-night and juggernaut damage is the suspected cause. "The problems of historic villages like ours are not being dealt with quickly enough," says Margaret Brown, chairman of Mayfield's amenity society. "They will be a mass of rubble populated by crippled neur-otics afraid to step out of their crumbling doorways if something doesn't stop the heavy lorries racing through them."

This picture shows the sort of problem juggernauts cause in small villages.

How the juggernauts bring hidden danger down Britain's streets

EVIDENCE that the life-expectancy of old buildings is shortened when they stand close to major roads is emerging from new research on traffic vibration which was not submitted to Sir Arthur Armitage's inquiry into heavy lorries and their environmental impact.

Although vibration damage is directly linked to the weight of vehicles, the Armitage team received only superficial information about it. The subject rated only 12 lines in the Transport Department's first submission to the inquiry; and in the second paper, further research was promised which is not in fact taking place. The department is itself strongly in favour of an increase in lorry weights above the present 32-ton maximum.

A full picture of the danger from traffic vibration will emerge next spring when James Crockett, a consulting engineer, presents his findings to the International Standards Organisation and the British Standards Institute.

His report will reveal that many medieval cathedrals and "greater churches" in Britain lean out on the side facing a heavy traffic flow, while the few that are traffic-free, such as the cathedrals of Peterborough, Canterbury, Norwich and St Albans, do not list at all.

The Chapter House of Lincoln Cathedral, close to the pounding of the A15, is now "settling" as much as 2mm in a single year after centuries of almost imperceptible movement. In some parts of York Minster, settlement has been nine times faster in the last 25 years than at any time in its life. "It is now quite usual to find settlement accelerating wherever there is traffic, after being fairly quiescent for centuries," says Crockett. All buildings more than 60 years old are liable to be affected.

He maintains that shifting and cracking will increase proportionately as vehicles become heavier, faster and more numerous – and as the state of Britain's roads deteriorates through poor maintenance.

"If there is just one bump outside a building, a tremendous shock is registered underground when a vehicle passes over it. Anything loose gets looser. Buildings assumed to be troublefree are going to have to be dealt with in two or three years' time."

Crockett rates groundborne and airborne vibration from traffic as more devastating than that caused by blasting and piledriving. "Damage is small each year and it is difficult to measure, but it goes on interminably. That is the damaging thing. Only after long research do you begin to see the pattern."

Crockett's findings, collected over 25 years, will embarrass the Transport Department, which has been playing down the effects of traffic vibration. In its submission to Armitage it concentrated on "disturbance to people" ("there is no reason to think that EEC-type vehicles would be worse in this respect") rather than on the structural consequences of vibration that can often be measured to a depth of 50ft. Groundborne vibration from heavy lorries, said the department, was "unlikely to be significant," except when the axles hit a bump.

Neither of the two government research establishments concerned with the question – the Transport and Road Research Laboratory and the Building Research Station – is now doing any work on vibration damage. The Civic Trust told the Armitage inquiry that ignorance was being used as "the reason for not compensating those who bear the cost and also for taking no steps to reduce the cost."

The Sunday Times 7.12.80

Now read this defence of the heavy lorry by Brian Fish. Mr Fish's arguments do not meet the criticisms put forward in the articles you have just read. What he does is to raise other points which we must take into account when we are trying to make up our minds on this issue. Read the article carefully, and, in note form, list the major points which Mr Fish makes.

CASE FOR THE JUGGERNAUT

SOME YEARS ago the word "Juggernaut" became attached to the heavy articulated lorry and identified it with that frightening figure of Hinduism; subsequently it has been the focal point of an emotional campaign against this vital servant of society.

In this campaign, some say that this type of vehicle should be taxed much more heavily, others that it should not be allowed at all. Let us consider these ideas.

First, why does this type of vehicle in fact exist?

The road haulage industry operates within what economists call the "perfect market." This means that those engaged in it can only remain in business if they provide the service which society at large demands of them. Providers of transport cannot either generate goods to be moved or decide how they will be moved.

More than 80 per cent of those with goods to be moved have found, after considering the alternatives in competitive terms, that the best way of getting their goods to their customers, whether they are intermediate producers or final consumers, is by road.

The cost of moving their goods to shops and warehouses must be such as to give them some hope of selling successfully in their own highly competitive markets.

We are now a greedy, acquisitive and consuming society which demands everything at the cheapest possible price. The modern articulated vehicle has evolved to play its vital role in just this cruelly competitive and demanding environment.

Supposing then that in pursuit of the idea that this vehicle should be taxed even more heavily, yet greater burdens of licence fees were placed upon it? The existing licence fee, increased by 30 per cent in the last budget to around £1,500 a year is likely to have added to it more than £3,000 a year in fuel for this vehicle.

Currently therefore, the cost of a typical maximum weight articulated vehicle approaches £100 per working day, including the wages of the driver, before the wheels start to turn, and approaching a further 30p per mile when they do.

Within these cost parameters the depressive influence of the market on charges is so massive that few, if any, vehicles engaged in general haulage are earning anything like the return on capital which could be enjoyed by putting the money in the market and leaving the goods to rot.

The return is far lower than it used to be when the industry was able to operate smaller, less sophisticated and cheaper vehicles under less rigid statutory regulations.

Thus, if we increase the tax, this is merely one more increase in operating costs which must find its way into the price of everything to be carried by that vehicle.

Supposing, further, that, as others suggest, this type of vehicle were banned altogether? These results can be anticipated:

● For every 32 tonne gross articulated vehicle on the road, we shall have to reconcile ourselves to two 16 tonne vehicles; those who complain of congestion will not like this.

● The average cost of goods carried by this alternative method will increase enormously: on a round trip of 200 miles this increase could be from around £7.50 per tonne to around £10.50 per tonne. Does society really want to inflict this sort of inflationary pressure on itself?

● The energy consumption per tonne thus carried would also increase unacceptably.

● A very large proportion of the goods we need are imported and, to pay for them, we have to export. Here again, to survive we have to be competitive, and this type of vehicle is vital in this role.

Although most of our Continental rivals use vehicles even larger than our own, we still have to compete with them both domestically and on the cross-Channel roll-on roll-off routes.

We also have to cope with our international container trades. These now account for more than 60 per cent of our trade – soon it will be 80 per cent. These containers, particularly those of 40ft in length, very often cannot be used to capacity because of weight restrictions in the UK compared with other countries. This imposes a cost penalty which is further aggravated when containers have to be reduced in weight before they can be legally taken on our roads. Only the modern articulated vehicle can take these containers. Thus to remove them from the scene would immediately and completely cripple our maritime trade.

• Many people suggest that this can all be overcome by transferring the goods to rail.

Every recent report, official or otherwise and confirmed by British Rail, concludes that this could not result in a reduction of more than 2 per cent in road-borne traffic.

Considerable volumes are already carried over the longer distances by rail where this is practical and competitive, and many containers are moved by the Freightliner system. A very small proportion, however, of those consigning or receiving goods, whether conventionally or in containers, has a rail connection; thus nearly all our goods have to be taken on the road at each end of the rail system.

Therefore to accuse the haulage industry of inflicting this vehicle as a burden on society is as ludicrous as it is unfair. The industry only survives by responding to the revealed economic requirements of society. It is therefore for society to decide, not merely whether it wants the heavy lorry as its servant, but more fundamentally whether it can or wishes to pay the economic price of changing the shape of this lorry into something less efficient, less able to compete in internation terms and less able to deliver the goods.

The Sunday Times 27.7.80.

☐ Finally, write an essay (400–500 words) in which you put forward your own opinions on what British policy should be towards the juggernaut.

Writing an argument

You have now read a number of passages which demonstrate the different techniques which a writer can use to persuade his readers to accept his point of view.

It was suggested on page 117 that there were in fact three main techniques:

☐ to use evidence which helps support your point of view

☐ to write in a forceful and persuasive manner

☐ to describe a relevant example or experience as vividly as you can

It is important to be aware of these different techniques so that when you are faced with an essay question which asks you to argue a particular case you can plan how best to tackle it.

☐ Consider, for instance, the following list of essay topics, all taken from recent examination papers. Think about each topic and write in note form answers to the following questions:

1 What is my point of view on this issue?

2 What do I know about the issue?

3 Have I any relevant experiences which I can describe?

4 Can I think of any forceful and persuasive points to make in support of my point of view?

5 How precisely am I going to use this knowledge and experience to persuade the reader to accept my point of view?

a) Package tours are a popular form of holiday. What are your views about them? (West Midland Examination Board, May 1977)

b) Horoscopes and fortune tellers – are they a service, an entertainment or a hoax? (JMB English Language Ordinary Level Paper B, June 1976)

c) There must always be one to command and others to obey. (Oxford and Cambridge, November, 1978)

d) Are the British too sentimental about animals? (Welsh Joint Education Committee, June, 1978)

e) To what extent do you think that society ought to look after its unemployed, its misfits, and its throwouts? Express your opinions fully, bearing in mind such aspects of the subject as our duty to help those less fortunate than ourselves, the individual's responsibility to himself and his dependents, and the financial burden of the Welfare State. (East Anglian Examination Board, April, 1978)

☐ Now choose one of these topics and develop your notes into an essay of around 400–500 words.

For further practice, either plan or actually write essays on the following topics.

a) Young people today can only follow the latest fashion.

b) Experiments on live animals are necessary if our medical knowledge is to develop.

c) Space exploration is a complete waste of time and money.

d) We live in a sick society where a pop singer can earn more in a night than a nurse in a year.

e) Schools should teach academic subjects like French and Physics and not involve themselves in areas like sex education which are the proper responsibility of the home.

Part B

Part B

Chapter One

Accurate and appropriate language

If you have studied Part A of this book you will know that we use language to do different things. Writing a description of a school disco, for instance, is not at all the same thing as writing an explanation of how to mend a puncture. In this chapter we are going to look in more detail at *four* of the ways in which we use language. Our aim is to help you with those aspects of language which students commonly find most difficult; when you have read this chapter you should feel more confident in your ability to write accurately and appropriately.

Introduction:
Checking the communication channel

When talking or writing to people it is obviously crucial that they are able to follow what we are saying or writing. This section looks at the different ways in which language can be used to allow communication to take place.

☐ Consider the predicament of the pilot in this cartoon.

He has an urgent message to communicate, but before he can do that he has to open up *the channel of communication*.

Look at a number of things he might say as he is talking to ground control:

Interference on line: can you repeat?

Over and out.   Z Victor Tango calling ground control . . .

Are you hearing me?   Receiving you strength R5.

Roger.

☐ Which of these is used for each of the following functions?

1 Opening up the channel
2 Checking that the communication channel is still open
3 Dealing with noise in the channel
4 Giving feedback to show that the channel is still open
5 Preparing to close the channel
6 Closing the channel

☐ Now look at the following expressions. Which of them performs each of the above functions?

1 'Well, we can't stand here all day.'
2 'Really?'
3 'Sorry, I didn't quite catch that.'
4 'Excuse me. . . .' (said when going up to someone in the street)
5 'See you next week, then.'
6 'Do you see what I mean?'

What these examples demonstrate is that *we often use language to open, maintain, and close the communication channel.*

So far you have been considering examples of *spoken* language. *Written* language is in some ways different. Are there any of the above six functions which do not occur in written language?

☐ What is the function of:

1 Big headlines in a newspaper
2 A postcard saying 'Wish you were here.'
3 The words 'The End.'
4 The word 'Finally . . .' at the beginning of a paragraph
5 An imaginative title for an essay

The word 'finally' in example number 4 is an example of what we can call *a linking signal*. A linking signal is a word or phrase which helps people understand what you are writing or saying by showing them how one idea leads on to the next. They are especially useful in practical writing. In conversation we can interrupt to ask the speaker what he means, but in writing we cannot, of course, do this. So in written language it is useful to have signposts or linking signals so that the reader does not have any problem in following the argument.

☐ Read the following dialogue. Write down all the linking signals and explain their function. They may, for example, be used to: make a new start, change the subject, interrupt, reinforce an argument, summarize, make a list of points, put what has been said in a different way, illustrate or expand an idea, contradict, and so on. The first signal here is 'Well', the second 'Firstly', and they work together to focus the staff's attention on the meeting.

Staff Meeting

Headmaster   Well, another term is beginning. Let's discuss this term's arrangements. Firstly, we have decided on some measures for keeping the pupils more usefully occupied. For example, we intend to increase homework to six hours a night and we intend to make them work much harder during lessons. Incidentally, Mr. Spiggot, have you ordered some more chalk? My billiard cue has begun to let me down. Now, the question of homework. . . .

Miss Sprockett   By the way, Headmaster, have we any news of the plans to rebuild the assembly hall?

Headmaster   With respect, Miss Sprockett, that is a curious question coming from you. To begin with, it was your pupils who knocked it down. Secondly, you did nothing to stop them. Moreover, you lent them the pickaxes. What is more, you personally drove the bulldozer. In short, I hold you chiefly responsible for the distressing end to our carol concert last term.

Miss Sprockett   3T don't like carols, Headmaster. Anyway, it was getting very stuffy in there.

Headmaster   In other words, Miss Sprockett, your policy of inciting 3T to guerrilla warfare is to continue?

Miss Sprockett   In a word, Headmaster, yes.

☐ Now write a paragraph which begins with sentence 1, and where each succeeding sentence begins with the linking signal indicated.

1 I have never really understood why teachers are obsessed with hard work.

2 Indeed ....

3 Moreover ....

4 However ....

5 For instance ....

6 Consequently ....

7 To conclude, ...

If you want people to understand what you are saying or writing, you must:

☐ command their attention

☐ help them with linking signals or signposts to understand your argument

☐ close the communication channel when you have finished.

Communicating information

This section concentrates on the problems which you face in trying to ensure that your reader understands exactly what you mean when you are attempting to tell him something or explain something to him.

1 Getting information

The remainder of the section will be concerned with *giving* information, but we shall begin by looking at ways of *getting* information.

The most obvious way is to ask a question, but not all questions are in fact requests for information. What is the function of each of these two utterances?

☐ How many other examples can you think of, of utterances which have the form of a question but which have some other function than that of asking for information? *Conversely,* asking direct questions may not always be the best way of getting the information we need. How many ways can you think of for asking how much you are going to be paid in your new job as a cinema usher(ette)?

For example: 'How much are you going to pay me?'

'I was wondering if you could possibly tell me how much I am going to be paid.'

☐ It is often important to avoid asking direct questions in writing. Can you rewrite this letter so that Arthur is more likely to get the job?

Dear Headmaster,

Can I have a job at your school? What are the pupils like? How do I get there? What sort of questions are you going to ask at the interview?

Yours sincerely
Arthur Glum

2 Making yourself understood

a Taking account of what the reader knows

It is always easy to assume that your audience knows as much about the subject you are writing or talking about as you yourself do. Often, of course, they do not, and your essays and stories will be much clearer and easier to understand if you always remember not to take anything for granted.

☐ Can you, for instance, understand what this woman is talking about?

No, the dog wasn't. But they were.

What information would you need to understand what she means? She has done three things which prevent us from understanding her:

She has *referred* to something that has gone before. (Which dog does she mean by 'the dog'? The person she is talking to knows, but we don't.)

She has *left things out*. (The dog wasn't what? They were what?)

She has *substituted* 'They' for a more explicit phrase naming the people in question. ('Mr. & Mrs. Crump', or 'The people who live next door to me', for example.)

What is she talking about anyway?

This is what led up to what she said.

In the first cartoon, the speaker assumes that the person to whom she is speaking knows about the dog jumping out of the car. If we do not know that this has happened then we cannot understand what she is talking about. It is important in your own writing that you do not make this mistake. Your reader can only understand the situation you are describing if you give her the necessary information.

When you write an explanation of something you should also bear in mind how much your reader *already* knows about whatever it is that you are explaining. If the reader is an expert, then you can take things for granted that you would have to explain to someone who is less well informed.

☐ Try, for instance, the following exercises.

1 You go to a football/tennis match every week with your friend Jim, who is an expert on the game. He is in hospital this week and has had to miss this week's match. Write and tell him what happened.

2 You have come to England from a country where there is no television or radio. You go to a football/tennis match for the first time in your life: you had never heard of the game before. Write home to your parents (who have never heard of the game either) and explain what happened.

3 Isabelle Lassègue has never been to England before. She is going to come and visit you. Write and explain to her how she must get from the nearest railway station to your house.

4 Christopher Davies knows your town (or village) very well, but has never actually been to your house. He lives close to your nearest railway station. Write and tell him how to get to your house.

b Referring and substituting

We use certain words as substitutes for the main subject we are writing about. These words are useful, but they can cause confusion.

☐ To alert you to this possible problem, read the following passage:

> Paris is a great beauty. As such it possesses all the qualities that one finds in any other great beauty: chic, sexiness, grandeur, arrogance, and the absolute inability and refusal to listen to reason. So if you're going there you would do well to remember this: no matter how politely or distinctly you ask a Parisian a question he will persist in answering you in French.
>
> Fran Lebowitz   *Metropolitan Life*

Can you say what you understood by the following words when you read the passage?

> such   it   there   this   he

Which of these words refer *back* to something already mentioned? Do any refer *forward*?

☐ Now read these sentences:

'My father's nose is medium-sized. But my mother's is enormous.'

'Has your mother finished her book yet?'

'Nearly. My father's finished his.'

What do you understand by?

> my mother's   nearly   his

These sentences demonstrate the way in which we take it for granted that we can leave things out in our speech and writing. The speaker here assumes that the person to whom he is speaking will understand that 'his', for instance, must refer to the book. If you do not make this assumption then your writing can seem clumsy and long-winded. But you must always remember that there are possibilities for confusion if it is not absolutely clear what you have omitted.

The following exercises will help you to understand this point.

☐ Rewrite these sentences so that the speaker or writer takes account of what has gone before in the conversation or text?

For example, the second sentence in number 1 can be reduced to 'I would like one' and the second sentence in number 2 to 'I think he is' or 'I think so'.

1 'I've got some bananas covered in chocolate sauce and treacle.'
  'I would like a banana covered in chocolate sauce and treacle.'

2 'Is David as silly as his brother?'
  'I think David's as silly as his brother.'

3 'Do you like driving my car?'
  'Yes I like driving your car.'

4 The dog ran away. The fact that the dog had run away made Miss Sludge very unhappy.

5 My garden is very untidy. Her garden is even more untidy.

6 She put a new engine in the car. I don't know how she put a new engine in the car.

7 Can you lend me a few drawing pins? I need a few drawing pins.

8 Whiskey and vodka are my favourite drinks, but whiskey isn't cheap and vodka isn't cheap either.

9 Piers and Miles both take me out to expensive restaurants, but I like Geoff better than Piers or Miles.

10 He isn't sure that he'll come tonight, but he may come tonight.

☐ If you look carefully at where the authors have referred forwards or back, left things out or substituted one word or phrase for another, you should be able to work out the original order of the sentences in these three paragraphs. In each case the first and last sentence are in the right place, but the sentences in the middle have been jumbled up.

Revolution

1 There were two versions of 'Revolution', but the underground left only picked up on the one that said 'Count me out'.

2 There was a third version that was just abstract, *musique concrète*, people screaming.

3 I put in both because I wasn't sure.

4 I thought I was painting in sound a picture of revolution – but I made a mistake, you know.

5 The original version which ends up on the L.P. said 'Count me in' too.

6 The mistake was that it was anti-revolution.

John Lennon from an interview in *Time Out*, 1980.

The Girl on the Train

1 Manning fell in love, in a way.

2 So was Manning himself, and almost everybody else in the carriage.

3 She was not, as he had envisaged, sunburnt and wearing a slight cotton dress.

4 It was on a suburban train, on the Mozhaisk line, and the girl was sitting in the seat opposite him.

5 She was pale, with very fair hair, and she was wearing a quilted anorak and thick trousers.

6 They were going on a rally or ramble organized by the Faculty Sport Club in the forest outside Moscow under Sasha's leadership.

Michael Frayn   *The Russian Interpreter*

Mechanical knowledge

1 So far we have said nothing about mechanical knowledge: how a car works.

2 This will not only make you a better driver, but add to your interest in driving.

3 There are a number of very useful books which explain simply how a car works.

4 It is not necessary to know all the complicated details of car construction to be a good driver.

5 It will also prolong the life of your car.

6 But the more you do know the better, because if you know how the different parts of a car work, and what happens when you use the controls, you will develop a sense of car sympathy.

7 It would repay you to get one of these and study it.

Department of Transport   *Driving*

☐ Write a paragraph made up of about seven sentences on *How to avoid people who try to make you do things you don't want to do*. Then rewrite it with the first and last sentences in the same place but the other sentences jumbled up. Give it to someone else and see if they can sort it out into its original order.

3   Organizing sentences

a   The construction of individual sentences

When we speak we take account of what the person we are speaking to already knows by stressing certain parts of the sentence.

☐ Look at two different ways in which Geoff Foster could present a piece of information to his wife:

In one of these cases Mr and Mrs Foster must already have been talking about Barcelona. Which?

It must be in the *first* case, because the emphasis falls on the last piece of *new* information in the sentence (or sense-group). Anything that comes after the emphasized word is *given*: the Fosters must already have been talking about Barcelona just before the part of the conversation shown in the second cartoon took place.

When we write we cannot use our voice to give emphasis, but we still have to take account of what is new information for our readers and what they already know. Normally we assume that a sentence is to be read as if the emphasis fell at the end (on the last noun, verb, adjective or adverb), so that the sentence: *Aunt Ethel's lodger wants to work in Barcelona* would be read as: Aunt Ethel's lodger wants to work in *Barcelona*. The new information will be assumed to be given by *Barcelona*, and perhaps by anything that has come before it in the sentence.

In spoken language we can focus attention on an earlier part of the sentence by using our voice to give emphasis. Supposing, for example, that Mrs Foster knows that Aunt Ethel's lodger is planning to do something in Barcelona but not that what he plans to do is work. Mr Foster will then say 'Aunt Ethel's lodger wants to *work* in Barcelona.' In written language we must find other devices for placing the emphasis where we want it.

☐ Look at these sentences and decide how much you think is *given* information already known by the readers and how much you think is *new*.

e.g. It was her neighbour who fell downstairs in the middle of the night.

Given: Someone fell downstairs in the middle of the night.

New: It was her neighbour.

1 What killed him was the cold.
2 It was his mother who used to knit his sweaters.
3 The person who came to dinner was my ex maths teacher.
4 It was the lodger who forgot to lock the back door.
5 The country she wants to visit most is Japan.

☐ Look at this sentence from spoken language:
   Hugo Loonbrain tore up Gillian's photograph.

Can you complete these sentences in written language so that the emphasis falls in the same place?

1 .... by Hugo Loonbrain.

2 It was ....

3 The person ....

☐ Now look at this sentence from spoken language:

Hugo Loonbrain *tore up* Gillian's photograph.

Can you complete this sentence in written language so that the emphasis falls in the same place?

What ....

☐ Here are some more sentences from spoken language. For each one, think of one or more ways of putting the sentence into written language so that the emphasis falls in the same place.

1 They *resprayed* the car.
2 *My* father told me about the empty whiskey bottles.
3 *The police* are interviewing my next-door neighbour.
4 He showed me a *photograph* of his six children.
5 The girl at the *front* kept interrupting the teacher.

b Writing more complex sentences

When you link sentences together you must decide what the relationship between the sentences is.

☐ Look at these two sentences:

I destroyed the photographs. I wanted to get revenge on Simon.

The relationship between them is one of *purpose*. This can be expressed by linking the two sentences together:

I destroyed the photographs to get revenge on Simon.

There are a number of other ways of expressing a relationship of purpose:

I left home so I wouldn't have to meet him at the bus stop every morning.

I threw away the letters in order to prove that he was no longer important to me.

I went abroad in order that he might never discover my whereabouts.

I came back so that I could make a fresh start.

☐ You have returned from America and the immigration officials want to know what the purpose of your visit was.

Give as many reasons as you can think of, and begin each one: 'I went there . . .'

Remember that when you use more *formal* links (like *in order that*) the rest of the sentence will need to be more formal.

143

☐ Now look at these sentences, which have a relationship of *cause*:

Mathilda hated shepherd's pie. She gave her dinner to the dog.

How many ways of expressing this relationship can you think of? These words and phrases may be useful:

because, so, on account of, out of hatred for . . ., hating . . .

☐   Arthur came home from the disco. He did his maths homework.

These two sentences already express a *time* relationship, simply by their order.

How many other ways of expressing this relationship can you think of?

☐ There are a number of other possible relationships by which sentences may be linked together: can you say which of the following sentences involve relationships of

    a) purpose

    b) cause

    c) time

    d) condition

    e) negative condition

    f) contrast

    g) addition

    h) alternatives

1 Jim had his hair permed to impress Julia.

2 If the teachers are on strike, the children are happy.

3 Although she liked playing with fire engines, everyone gave her dolls for Christmas.

4 Knowing that Aunt Marjorie was due to arrive, George left the house.

5 Unless you water the plants the leaves will drop off.

6 Not only does he play the violin for the Royal Philharmonic Orchestra, he also plays in goal for Queens Park Rangers.

7 Either we could have dinner at the Ritz or I could bring some ham sandwiches.

8 Having arrived at the station, he burst into tears.

9 If they don't come soon I'm going to rip those pipes out myself.

10 In spite of the fact that he is unemployed, he still believes in the government's policies.

☐ Finally can you write two versions of the life story of Alfonso Ripamonti? The first one should be very formal, as it will be used for his official biography. The second should be very informal: as told to you by Alfonso's friend Lou.

1 (Time relationship)	Alfonso born. Alfonso's father killed in an accident.
2 (Causal relationship)	No work in Italy. Alfonso comes to England.
3 (Relationship of purpose)	Alfonso trains as a hairdresser. Wants to meet famous people.
4 (Condition)	He tells them they have nice hair. They give him big tips.
5 (Negative condition)	He doesn't eat much. He can send money back to his mother in Bologna.
6 (Contrast)	He works very hard. André of Mayfair dismisses him.
7 (Addition)	He has no job. His wife leaves him.
8 (Alternatives)	He finds another job as a hairdresser. He retrains as a plumber.

Remember, since you cannot use your voice in written language to emphasize new information, you need to think about how best you can *order* the words in a written sentence so that the emphasis falls at the right moment in the sentence. In joining simple sentences together it is the relationship between the sentences which determines the linking words which you should choose.

---

4 Organizing paragraphs

If you organize your writing into paragraphs you will help your reader to understand the point which you are making. It is, for instance, the use of short paragraphs in the article on smoking on page 107 which makes the article easy to follow. In thinking about paragraphs you need to consider *both* the structure of your essay as a whole *and* the structure of individual paragraphs. This section looks at some of the ways in which it is possible to organize ideas *within* a paragraph.

☐ Read the three paragraphs which follow and think about the order in which the writers have chosen to present their facts and arguments.

1 The ways in which the mass media reinforce gender roles are insidious and pervasive. The images they present reflect and exploit society's definition of gender roles. To take just one example, it is enlightening to compare Polish and American women's magazines in the early 1950s. In the American magazines the idealised woman was young, feminine, domesticated, pursuing a man, or (if she already had one) devoted to the care of home and children. The Polish stereotype showed women as economically equal with men rather than parasitic on them, as not having a different role within the family and as attracting men by their success at work. This was the official Polish ideology on the family at that time.

Ann Oakley   *Sex, Gender and Society*

145

2 In 1938 two per cent of our national income was spent on advertising. This proportion dropped sharply during the war, but has risen steadily in the post-war period to over 2.1 per cent in 1963. European countries spend less proportionately on advertising than we do, but the comparable figure for The United States is considerably higher (2.7 per cent in 1963). Another interesting way of looking at these figures is to compare the annual amount each country spends on advertising for each member of its population. A 1970 survey estimated this at 89.56 dollars per head in the United States, as compared with 21.31 dollars or £8.90 per head in the United Kingdom. The indications are that the more prosperous a country becomes the more it spends proportionately on advertising, though which is cause and which effect is a moot question. The probability is that the proportion of our national resources which we in Great Britain devote to advertising (already high comparatively) will continue to increase in the future.

Frank Whitehead *Advertising*

3 TV newsreading is, on the surface, a more or less humdrum *métier*. Given an appearance this side of a joke-shop mask, an ability to read the outcome without your eyes darting about like disturbed minnows, and a constant pronunciation, not necessarily correct, of foreign names and places, it should be anybody's bag. In fact our newscasters are chosen as carefully as the characters in a long-running soap opera. They have become more important to us than the disasters they relay; the much-cherished Cassandras of the electronic market-place.

George Melly *The Media Mob*

Paragraph 1   begins with a generalization. This is followed by a sentence which elaborates and clarifies that generalization. The remainder of the paragraph consists of exemplification.

Paragraph 2   is structured quite differently: a series of facts is followed by a conclusion.

Paragraph 3   has a different structure again: the first half of the paragraph expounds one idea and the second half offers an opposing point of view.

☐ Look at the following paragraphs and decide how the structure of each of them could be described.

What exactly do the television programmers mean when they speak of 'family entertainment'? Ideally, the phrase conjures up a cosy picture of the nuclear family clustered happily around their set, sharing a common pleasure in a spectacle catering for, and confirming, their mutual tastes and outlooks. In practice though, it's a lot more likely to mean some formula which is either actively

146

pleasing, or at least inoffensive, to those who control the channel change switch during peak viewing hours. Audience dictates content: and he who pays the rental calls the tune.

Andrew Weiner   *Family Man*

Thursday, 8 November. Day broke on a city in the wildest excitement and confusion, a whole nation heaving up in long hissing swells of storm. Superficially all was quiet; hundreds of thousands of people retired at a prudent hour, got up early and went to work. In Petrograd the streetcars were running, the stores and restaurants open, theatres going, an exhibition of paintings advertised . . . All the complex routine of common life – humdrum even in war-time – proceeded as usual. Nothing is so astounding as the vitality of the social organism – how it persists, feeding itself, clothing itself, amusing itself, in the face of the worst calamities.

John Reed   *Ten Days that Shook the World*

The appeal to recognition is important in soap opera. Yes, we say to ourselves, that's exactly how we'd expect such a family to behave. *The Archers* offers city dwellers a picture of the way they, the townsmen, expect country people to behave. What's more, these fictionalized characters behave in the way country people imagine *themselves* to behave. And the same applies to *Coronation Street*. 'That's exactly what it must be like,' says the green-belt suburbanite. 'That's what it *used* to be like,' says the viewer in the new Manchester high-rise flats. And the dwindling numbers of people who still live in *Coronation Street* see themselves as quaint and interesting – rough, but with hearts of gold.

Albert Hunt   *Shadows of Reality*

☐ Now try and write a paragraph like paragraph 1. Begin with the following generalization:

The ways in which schools . . . . are . . . . and . . . .

Then add a sentence elaborating on your meaning. (You could begin: That is to say that . . . or, In other words . . .)

Then give a series of examples to strengthen your point.

☐ Now try a paragraph like paragraph 2. Begin with a series of facts demonstrating that an increasing number of women are rejecting their traditional role. Start the last-but-one sentence: The indications are . . .

Start the last sentence: The probability is . . .

☐ Now try a paragraph like paragraph 3. Begin with an assertion: Vandalism is, on the surface, a . . .

Spend the first half of the paragraph supporting this assertion.

Then begin a sentence: In fact . . . and continue by putting an opposing viewpoint.

5 Clichés

A phrase such as 'Wish you were here' is a cliché: a 'stereotyped expression, a commonplace phrase' (Oxford English Dictionary). Such expressions are often called 'tired and stale', and their use is said to show 'mental laziness'. In a piece of imaginative writing or in any writing where you are putting forward your own viewpoint, they are clearly out of place, since they do not represent your own perceptions. In general the more clichés you use the more predictable and therefore boring your writing will become. As a demonstration of the *predictability* that results from reliance on clichés, see if you can fill in the gaps in this passage:

Ladies and Gentlemen, a new age is d _____ . The days of this government are n _____ . My party has an e _____ desire to make the world a better p _____ in which to l _____ . We shall explore every a _____ and leave no stone u _____ . If necessary we shall go to the e _____ of the e _____ in our quest for the l _____ at the end of the t _____ . I mean this from the b _____ of my h _____ .

☐ Look back to page 26, where different ways of approaching descriptive essays are discussed. Because they are *predictable*, clichés cannot be effective in conveying new information; because they are *familiar* they are unlikely to have a powerful effect on the reader; and because they consist of *ready-made phrases* they cannot define your personal attitude to what you are describing. See if you can find ways of rewriting these clichés so that they achieve the stated aim in each case.

1 Although he could hardly believe his eyes, he didn't turn a hair.
(Convey in a memorable way someone's controlled reaction to a shocking sight.)

2 I will stay by your side through thick and thin until we have weathered the storm.
(Convince someone that they can be certain of your support in a crisis.)

3 After Leroy went out of my life there was an aching void in my heart.
(Describe how upset you were by Leroy's departure.)

☐ Now write a passage describing life on a tropical island, using as many clichés as you can.

In Part A Chapter Two you learned ways of bringing to life the people that you write about. Using clichés to describe people has the opposite effect: it makes them into cardboard cut-outs.

☐ Look at these descriptions: which do you think rely on clichés, and which are more perceptive and accurate?

1 about Eamonn Andrews
Whether by design or because he can't help it, he wins over his audience by creating an embarrassing tension.

2 about Clark Gable
Softened by love perhaps but consistently and stubbornly *all* man, the devil-may-care adventurer.

3 about Paul McCartney
The Beatle with the cheeky cherubic good looks.

4 about Cliff Richard
He was showbiz's favourite convert, just a shade magisterial but untouched by any breath of scandal.

5 about Rudolf Valentino
The idol of the silver screen, a figure of romantic menace with brooding eyes.

☐ Think of five famous people. What are the clichés most often used to describe each of them? Can you think of ways of describing each of the five people that you have thought of that avoid clichés and try to be as accurate as possible?

☐ Write a story about either gangsters or cowboys and use as many clichés as you can to describe the characters.

Clichés do, however, have one function. Consider the phrase 'Wish you were here' on a postcard. Writing this phrase does not show any great originality of thought but in the context of a postcard it is not meant to. What it does do is reassure the receiver of the card that the communication channel is still open. We may not always need or want to express our personal feelings, and the use of a clichéd expression can be a useful way of showing that we are on friendly terms with someone when this is what the situation requires.

☐ Draw a line down the centre of a page. On one side, write a reassuring letter to an aunt whose dog has just died. Use clichés where you think it is appropriate ('everything is for the best' . . . etc.). On the other side write a letter giving your real feelings about both her and the dog. (Do you really hope she is well? Do you really want her to give your regards to cousin Peter?)

There are, then, some circumstances in which clichés can be highly functional.

Narrative

Many stories by inexperienced writers are difficult to follow because of a failure to understand and manage time relationships. This section will help you to understand what is involved in this aspect of writing.

1 Time relationships

☐ English uses some quite complicated ways of expressing relationships between past, present and future. To prove to yourself that you *can* understand these relationships read the following passage and answer the questions which follow.

> Smokey Joe was quietly sipping his bourbon in the saloon, where Belle had been singing her new number. If Jesse were here, he thought, he would have enjoyed hearing that. He should have been here by now.
>
> Curly had arrived, and he would have had a long tedious wait if he had not whiled away the time talking to Belle. Curly loved Belle. She had loved him, too. He would spend hours gazing at her across the saloon.
>
> Jake would be along later. He was the boss, and he had the plans for the bank. The whole gang was to meet at sundown. When they were all together they would ride off into the sunset.

1 Which of the gang were already in the Saloon?

2 Which of the gang had not yet arrived?

3 Whom was Smokey Joe expecting next?

4 Had Joe finished his bourbon?

5 Was Belle singing?

6 What was Curly doing?

7 Does Curly love Belle? Does Belle love Curly?

8 When did Curly gaze at Belle across the Saloon?

9 What can you tell about the time of day when Joe was sipping his bourbon?

10 What will happen when the gang meet?

☐ Write the opening paragraphs of a story, introducing various time relationships. Choose either:

A boy is waiting for his girlfriend, who is late. He is thinking about the
things that have happened, how they met, and about what they plan to
do.

Two old people sitting on a park bench reminisce and talk about the
people they see in the park.

Devise some questions on what you have written, asking about the time
relationships. Answer each other's questions.

2 Past, present and future

We need to be able to talk about the past, the present and the future.
Imagine time as a line:

PAST ←——————————————|——————————————→ FUTURE
                PRESENT MOMENT

We may want to talk about any part of this line – one point of it, a
segment of it, or the whole line.

English enables us to do this in various ways.

1 We can change the tense of the verb:

Present Tense	**Past Tense**
they *play* tennis	they *played* tennis
he *swims* well	he *swam* well
I feel miserable	I *felt* miserable
she *is* a mechanic	she *was* a mechanic

(Most verbs simply add *-ed* to make the past tense. A few, like *swim* and
feel, change the vowel sound.)

2 We can add bits of other verbs (mostly *be* and *have*) in various ways:

they *are playing* tennis

he *was swimming*

I *have been feeling* miserable

she *was to be* a mechanic

3 We can add other words which refer to specific bits of time:

they *play* tennis *on Saturdays*

he *swims* in the hundred metres *tomorrow*

I *feel* miserable *when I have a cold*

she *was* a mechanic *for three years*

We usually talk about past time by using past tense verbs, and about any
part of time which includes the present moment by using present tense

151

verbs. When it comes to talking about future time, we have a number of ways to choose from:

> he *swims* in the 400 metre relay tomorrow
>
> he *will swim* in the freestyle leg
>
> he *is swimming* at 3pm
>
> he *is going to swim* the race of his life

3   Keeping the time reference constant

One problem in writing is keeping the time reference constant. It is clearer if we imagine time as a line extending either side of the present moment in these diagrams.

In *narrative* writing you are talking about the past, so your writing should be in the *past tense*.

PAST ← _____ → FUTURE
events of story   PRESENT

☐ Write a paragraph about a childhood memory. Use the past tense.

In writing *argument*, you will be making generalizations and statements of your views which we can see as true for all time, past, present and future. You should therefore write in the *present tense*.

PAST ← _____ FUTURE
          PRESENT

☐ Write a paragraph on the differences between the sexes. Use the present tense.

If you make predictions, thus referring to future time, you can choose from the various ways of expressing future time in English.

PAST ← _____ → FUTURE
          PRESENT   Tomorrow and
                    tomorrow and

☐ Write a horoscope for your best friend for the next week. Try to use at least *three* different ways of expressing future time.

Narrative is usually in the past tense. It is about some point in time located in the past, told by someone located in the present moment.

PAST ← —————————————— → FUTURE
        point of   STORY TELLER
        story

If you want to talk about events which happened before or after the point of the story, you will need to adjust your choice of verb forms.

Thus, to refer to the *past in the past*:

John *had been* lonely and miserable until the day he *met* Jane.

PAST ← —————————————— → FUTURE
    john   john   STORY TELLER
    lonely   met jane

and to refer to the *future in the past*:

We *said* goodbye, but little did I know that I *was to see* him again soon.

PAST —————————————— → FUTURE
    we said   I saw   STORY TELLER
    goodbye him again

4 Reporting speech

When you report what someone has said the same kind of shift occurs. The actual words spoken may be in the present tense, but when they are reported, they are reported in the past tense (reported speech is sometimes called indirect speech).

☐ Read this dialogue. Write the policeman's report of the conversation to be read out in court at the trial of Kevin Jones. Begin: 'I approached the accused and asked him what his name was. He replied that . . .'

'Excuse me, sir,' the policeman said. 'What is your name?'

'It's Kevin Jones. Why do you want to know?' the man replied.

'Just routine enquiries, sir. What have you got in that sack you're carrying, sir?'

'It's some old clothes for the school jumble-sale,' Kevin answered.

'And where are you going with it, sir?' the constable enquired.

'I'm taking it to the school hall.'

'Do you mind showing me, sir?'

'No, of course I don't.' Kevin sheepishly opened the sack.

'Hello, hello, hello! I see there are some silver candlesticks nestling among the jumble, sir! I shall have to ask you to accompany me to the station.'

5 The relationship between time and tense

It is by no means always true in English that

present tense = present time
past tense   = past time

☐ Look at these examples. They each have the same verb in a present tense. Can you say what the time reference of each is (i.e. what part of the time line it refers to)?

1 I'm going to the cinema (said as you leave the room).

2 I'm going to the cinema tomorrow.

3 I'm going to the cinema far too often these days.

☐ Here are some more examples. For each one
identify the tense as *past* or *present* and
try to say what the *time reference* is. It could be:

    a moment in the past

    the present moment

    a period in the past continuing up to the present

    all time

    a future period

1 Water *boils* at 100°C.

2 My holiday *starts* tomorrow.

3 I *wondered* if you would like to come to my party.

4 You're smoking! I *thought* you'd given it up!

5 And Snow *comes* in from the pavilion end . . .

6 Rain *is coming* in from the west.

7 *Do* you *come* here often? Yes, I *come* here every Thursday.

8 I *blend* the eggs and sugar . . .

9 *Did* you *want* to see me?

10 I *was going* to London tomorrow, but I've had to cancel it.

11 The biscuits *will be* in the cupboard if you want any.

12 I *forget* what the plan was.

☐ Notice that one of the functions of the past tense is to express politeness, nothing to do with time at all. In which of the above sentences is it used in that way?

Even though we have said that narrative should be written in the past tense, writers of narrative quite often switch tenses for particular reasons:

> they may want to make a generalization which is true for all time
>
> they may predict what will happen next (future in the past)
>
> they may refer to an event that happened before the main narrative events (past in the past).

☐ Look at this extract from *Right Ho, Jeeves* by P. G. Wodehouse. Some of the verbs have been underlined. For each one, say

> what its *time reference* is
>
> why you think the author has used it rather than the simple past.

Bertie Wooster has found himself walking in the evening with the sentimental and romantic Madeleine Bassett:

1   There was a fag-end of sunset still functioning. Stars were beginning to peep out, bats <u>were fooling</u> round, the garden was full of
2   the aroma of those niffy white flowers which only <u>start</u> to put in their heavy work at the end of the day and it was plain that this was having the worst effect on her. Her eyes were enlarged, and her whole map a good deal too suggestive of the soul's awakening for comfort.

       Her aspect was that of a girl who was expecting something fairly fruity from Bertram.

3   In these circs., conversation inevitably flagged a bit. I <u>am</u> never at my best when the situation seems to call for a certain
4   soupiness, and <u>I've heard</u> other members of the Drones say the
5   same thing about themselves. I <u>remember</u> Pongo Twistleton telling me that he was out in a gondola with a girl by moonlight once, and the only time he spoke was to tell her that old story about the chap who was so good at swimming that they made him a traffic cop in Venice.

       Fell rather flat, he assured me, and it wasn't much later when the girl said she thought it was getting a little chilly and how about pushing back to the hotel.

6,7   So now, as I <u>say</u>, the talk rather hung fire. It <u>had been</u> all very well for me to promise Gussie that I would cut loose to this girl about aching hearts, but you want a cue for that sort of thing. And when, toddling along, we reached the edge of the lake and she
8   finally spoke, <u>conceive</u> my chagrin when I discovered that what she was talking about was stars.

       Not a bit of good to me.

P. G. Wodehouse   *Right Ho, Jeeves*

Conveying attitudes

What you say or write can convey a lot about your attitude. It is important to be able to give the right impression, and not to convey an attitude that you don't intend. A good writer can *imply* a great deal that is not said in so many words, if he or she is aware of the way language can suggest attitudes and feelings. In the sections below we will see how:

1 You can tell your readers something about your feelings towards your subject, the things you are writing about: *attitude to the subject*.

2 You can convey to your audience what you think about *them*, even if you do not make any direct personal comments: *attitude to the reader*.

3 You can suggest something about your attitude to what you are writing itself, the message you are sending: *attitude to the message*.

1 Attitude to the subject

Your attitude to the things you are talking or writing about can be conveyed in several ways. The most obvious way is in the words you choose. Many words refer to the same things but have different *connotations*, that is, they suggest different attitudes.

Here are some parts of words which refer to similar things or qualities, but with different connotations:

Positive	Negative
up-to-date	newfangled
cautious	cowardly
brave	foolhardy
determined	stubborn

☐ Here are some more words and phrases. Arrange them into pairs referring to similar things, and write them in the appropriate columns, as above.

obstinate	gaudy	calculating	increased
shrewd	firm	traditional	unemployment
skinny	old fashioned	elitism	pursuit of
increased leisure	colourful	slim	excellence

Add some more pairs to the list if you can.

☐ Choose three pairs of words from the completed list. For each pair, write two newspaper headlines for the same news story, using one word from the pair in each, to convey different attitudes. For example:

> Chancellor Stands Firm over Tax on Air
>
> Treasury Obstinate over Breathing Levy.

☐ Using the information given on the three characters below, write a paragraph describing each in a favourable light. Then rewrite your three paragraphs, giving the same facts but conveying an unfavourable attitude.

> Rick Spink, rock singer, age 19, ex bank-clerk, band called the Sparx, first record ('I can't speak') reached No. 37 in charts, wears yellow jumpsuit, about to tour USA.
>
> Dr Marion Hughes, M.P., Labour Member for Welsh constituency, Shadow Minister for Health Service, campaigned for equal pay for women, rides a bike.
>
> Sir Humphrey Coldstream, managing director, Crunchybix Dogfood Co. Ltd., drives Rolls-Royce, plays squash, has five children, member of R.S.P.C.A.

2 Attitude to the reader

There are several ways of showing your attitude to your readers, without saying anything directly about them.

When you speak, you can express your attitude to the person you are speaking to partly by intonation, that is, the way your voice goes up and down in pitch (its 'tune', as it were).

For example, the sentence, 'Close the door' can be said in a way which means:

> I order you to close the door
> I want you to close the door – and I expect you to do so
> Please close the door
> Shall I close the door?
> Did you say, 'Close the Door?'
> Was it the *door* that you wanted me to close?
> Did you mean *close* the door, not open it?
> I've told you once – close the door!

☐ Try saying the sentence 'close the door.' with the meanings above. If you can, ask someone else to identify which meaning you intend.

This works for speech, but when you write, you have to be able to make all these meanings clear in what you write; you can't be sure that your readers will read what you've written with the same intonation as you intended, so you have to make the attitude explicit in the writing.

□ Think of and practise all the different ways you can say each of the following sentences.

□ Write out several versions of each sentence to make the differences in attitude explicit, in the way we have done above for 'Close the Door'.

1 Really.

4 I think so.

2 Your name is on the list.

5 Don't do that again.

3 It's snowing again.

6 It's very cheap.

One of the main ways of conveying your attitude to your audience is by adjusting the level of *formality* with which you talk to them. Most of the essays you write in an examination will be fairly formal, and it is important to be aware of when your language is becoming informal, because this may be inappropriate for the kind of essay you want to write. Some features of language at the informal end of the spectrum are often described as slang or colloquialisms, and are usually thought to be out of place in an examination essay, except perhaps in dialogue. (They are of course appropriate in some situations in spoken language.) However, it is just as possible to write inappropriately by being too *formal* (which can sound pompous). For example, if you, or a character in a story, wants to borrow some money from a friend, it would be very odd, even wrong, to say or write:
'I have insufficient resources for the purchase of refreshments.'

It would be much better to have the character say (just as you would be more likely to say):
'I haven't enough cash to buy a Coke.'

□ Make a list of all the possible ways you can think of to address a stranger whose name you don't know. For each one, think of a situation in which it might be used, and a situation in which it definitely wouldn't.

	Used	*Not used*
Sir	Pupil to new teacher	Customer to shop assistant
Mate		
Hey you		
Young lady		

How *formal* or *informal* you sound depends on a number of things. It depends partly on particular words, and partly on the sentence constructions you choose.

Here are some pairs of words which refer (roughly speaking) to the same thing, but differ in degree of *formality*.

Neutral or informal	*Formal*
friendly	amicable
live	reside
drinks	refreshments
cash	resources

158

☐ Sort these words into pairs of roughly similar meaning, and list in two columns *formal* and *informal*, as above.

dwelling	hide
eat	request
pay	boss
restorative	remuneration
talk	superior
home	ask
discourse	consume
tonic	conceal

In the example above (asking for a loan) it was the actual words which made a difference. When we made the sentence more formal, we kept the same construction.

☐ Rewrite these sentences, keeping the same grammatical shape and changing some of the individual words. Make the first three more formal, and the next three more informal.

1 I meant to ask you about your holiday.

2 Hang on a minute and I'll give him a ring.

3 You'll have to change your plans, I'm afraid.

4 You are requested to attend at 3pm prompt.

5 I have been notified that my great-aunt's decease is imminent.

6 I was proceeding along High Street in the normal course of my duties when I observed the accused engaged in extracting the wallet from the witness's handbag.

☐ Now look at this sentence:

The maturity value of your contract will not be known until payments are complete and the related movements of the Retail Prices Index have been calculated and published.

Save As You Earn (SAYE)

Here both the structure and the individual words create a formal style.

☐ Compare these versions. In the first, the grammatical structure only has been changed, using the same vocabulary.

In the second, both the vocabulary and the structure have been changed.

'We will not know the maturity value of your contract until you have completed the payments and we have calculated and published the related movements of the Retail Prices Index.'

'We will not know how much your contract will be worth at the end of it until you have finished paying and we have worked out and published the changes in the Retail Prices Index which are connected with it.'

☐ Rewrite the following passage in an informal style, changing both vocabulary and grammatical structure.

Restrictions on new contracts

16 A person shall not enter into a savings contract –
   a) if the starting date under the contract would be less than a month (or such other period as the Treasury may from time to time determine) after the starting date under another savings contract entered into by him; or
   b) if the aggregate of each monthly contribution which would be payable under the contract, and of each monthly contribution payable under any other savings contracts of the Third Issue under which he is making payments would exceed £20, or such greater sum as the Treasury may from time to time determine.
   Any sums paid by a person under a contract entered into in breach of this paragraph shall be repaid to him without any bonus (whether Index-linked or fixed) or interest. Three months' notice of any determination of the Treasury under this paragraph shall be given in the London, Edinburgh and Belfast Gazettes.

SAVE AS YOU EARN OFFICE, DURHAM   1 JULY 1975

☐ Take a copy of your school rules. Rewrite them as informally as possible. This will mean, for example:

   using personal pronouns (you, we, I), and
   using colloquial or everyday language.

Now rewrite them as formally as you can. This will mean, for example:

   no personal pronouns, and
   using difficult, obscure or unusual words.

For each version, try to say what the implications would be if the rules *were* written in that way. What would it suggest about the relationships between the makers of the rules and those who are subject to them? What *attitudes to the reader* does each version imply?

3   Attitude to the message

You can help your readers to see what your attitude is by helping them with certain signposts in your writing.

These signposts actually tell your reader something about your attitude to what you've written: the message you are sending itself.

For example:

> *To my surprise,* I found it quite easy to learn to drive.
> *Even more important,* I seemed to be quite good at it.
> There were times when I was flustered, *obviously.*
> *However,* I only crashed the car once.
> *Unfortunately,* this was in the middle of my driving test.
> I failed, *needless to say.*

If you try reading this without the signposts, you will find it much more difficult.

Other signposts of a similar kind include:

> Understandably, wisely, to be sure, which is not surprising (in view of –), what is more remarkable is that . . ., to our regret, evidently, of course, in fact, undoubtedly, perhaps, possibly, apparently, actually, ideally, admittedly, surely, presumably, supposedly, plainly, officially, in theory, basically, surprisingly, probably, clearly.

☐ Add an appropriate signpost to each sentence in the following dialogue which will help the reader understand the speaker/writer's attitude.

A Her tennis is improving, _____ .

B _____ her service is very powerful.

A The backhand needs some practice _____ .

B _____ she's greatly improved this season.

A _____ it's because of her new partner.

B He's been a great encouragement _____ .

A Plenty of disco dancing _____ has helped keep her fit.

B I'm playing her in the final _____ .

A I wish you luck then!

Instructing and persuading

One of the things we use language for is to get other people to do things. This may take the form of *instructions* to perform various tasks, or it may be *persuading* people to share your point of view or to act in a certain way. The latter includes all kinds of argument and discussion, political persuasion and campaigning. It is important to use the right kind of language, according to the situation.

1 Instructing

☐ Look at this list. It shows a number of different ways of asking someone to open the window.

> [Point to a closed window]
> Will you open the window, please?
> I wonder if you would be so good as to open the window?
> Open the window!
> Would you mind opening the window, please?
> I'd be very glad if you could possibly manage to open the window.

Put these six versions in rank order according to

> how polite you judge them to be (least polite first)
> how indirect they are (most direct request first)

Is there any relationship between your two lists?

What is it?

What conclusions can you draw from this?

☐ You are in a café, and you want to order a coke. Here are a number of ways in which you might do it.

1 [No words. You simply point at an actual Coke, *or* at the words on the menu.]
2 Coke!
3 A Coke, please.
4 I wonder if I could have a Coke, please?
5 Would you mind terribly bringing me a Coke?
6 Fetch me a Coke.
7 Could I have a Coke please?
8 I'd like a Coke, please.
9 Isn't anyone serving Coke around here?
10 I'd like a glass of cool, fizzy, tongue-tingling, refreshing Coke.
11 One of those, please.
12 10 fluid ounces of a carbonated fluid containing sugar, permitted flavouring and colouring . . .

13 I say! A spot of Coke would be most awfully jolly!

14 Oy mate! Fetch us a Coke, eh?

Consider which of these you could use to order a Coke. Fill in a chart like this one for each item.

Could it be used to order Coke in a café	Could it be used to ask for Coke in another situation? If so what?	What attitude to the waiter is conveyed?	Could it be used in talking about Coke in another situation? If so what?
Yes, but unlikely	In a pub if very noisy	Rude, curt	
Yes, if waiter far away		Rude aggressive	Asking someone else if they want a coke

Which version would you be most likely to use?

☐ Choose one of the following: Think of all the possible ways of asking someone to:

    return a ball which has landed in their garden
    pass on a message to a friend whom you want to telephone you that night
    pass the gravy at the dinner table

Give each version of the request marks out of ten for:

how indirect you are being	(1 = very direct; 10 = very indirect)
how polite you are being	(1 = very impolite; 10 = very polite)

You will find information about writing instructions in Section A, page 112, and in Communicating information, page 136, where we discuss ways of making the language of instructions clear and sufficiently explicit for your audience.

2 Persuading

Many writers and speakers want to convince their audience of certain things, influence their opinions, persuade them to vote in a certain way, and so on. Equally, many different kinds of language can be used for this:

    slogans
    logical reasoned arguments
    threats
    expressions of personal feeling
    parliamentary language
    and so on.

☐ Consider all these ways of trying to persuade someone not to vote for your political opponent.

1 If you do, I'll dot you one.

2 2–4–6–8–

Who will we exterminate?

A–D–A–M–S Adams!

3 Voters for Mr Adams will be prosecuted.

4 No voting for Mr Adams.

5 Please do not vote for Mr Adams.

6 There are many reasons why the election of Mr A. would be a disaster for this country's ailing economy. Firstly, . . .

7 Voting for Mr Adams is an offence punishable by garrotting.

8 I hate him. He's got big ears.

9 Would *you* buy a used car from this man?

10 The Right Honourable Gentleman is proposing a course which can only lead to increased unemployment. If this bill goes through, chaos will ensue . . .

11 And so, brothers, I urge you to join me in the struggle against this man Adams . . .

For each one answer the following questions. Again, the answers can be set out in chart form.

Could it be used to persuade not to vote?	Is the language used for persuasion in another context?	In what context would you expect it to be used?
No		As a physical threat
No	Yes - football supporters	

☐ You are going to attempt to persuade people to share a view you hold strongly.

For example: that all schools should be single-sex

that smoking in public places should be banned

that public transport should be free

You may well have views on other matters you want to write about.

Write three separate paragraphs on the same topic, attempting to persuade people to share your views, each addressed to a different audience. Your language should be appropriate to the audience and function you have in mind. Select from this list, or think of your own:

part of a letter to your M.P. who is about to vote on the matter

part of a script of a speech to be delivered at a public meeting

what you might say to an unconvinced friend

the text of a poster for display in public

part of a leader article in a popular newspaper

In Chapter Five on *Argument* it was said that a writer could try to persuade through the force of his language (page 118). What does this mean? Look again at this passage:

> Man has come to <u>dominate</u> the earth and to prosper by his <u>clever-ness</u>. With the tools and technological knowledge now at his command, he not only <u>tinkers</u> with his environment to make it more comfortable – he rapes it. We continue, nevertheless, to use <u>brute force</u> to make natural resources yield up what we want – now – from them. Danger signals <u>blink</u> urgently on all sides. Our survival really is in the balance.
>
> Rachel Carson   *Silent Spring*

☐ Consider the underlined words. See if you can find alternatives for each one which would be more neutral. You need to choose words with a similar meaning but without the implications of the words in the original. It is the implications which the words possess which carry the persuasive force.

What is the effect of the passage if you substitute all your neutral alternatives?

It is not always possible to substitute neutral alternatives for loaded words in persuasive writing. Some writers state their judgements more explicitly, hoping their readers will agree; some words are used to express an opinion directly, rather than indirectly through their implications. The following letter, for instance, contains a number of examples of such direct expression of opinion. Can you pick them out?

I would like to protest very strongly against Roger Woddis's recent cowardly verbal attack ('Woddis On . . .', 17–23 January) against John Lennon.

Woddis's bitter salvo is as pathetic as it is risible. It resembles an embittered attack against a famous lyricist by an obscure one. The writer accuses Lennon of having been an egoist, a Jekyll and Hyde, mindless and 'pain-vaunting'.

Well, maybe he was – at the beginning. But later he discovered the value of life. Woddis sneers when Lennon is called a saint, but he did more for peace, justice and the world in general than Woddis, with his petty small-minded vindictiveness, can hope to achieve.

Peter Thorndike
Christchurch, Dorset

Radio Times 7th–13th February 1981

165

In this final example the writer gives two versions of the same situation, each attempting to create opposite attitudes. Write down the words in the first paragraph which carry unfavourable implications, and those in the second which carry favourable implications.

WITHIN five years several oil production platforms may have to be shut down to allow major repairs to take place – with unpleasant conse- quences for the balance of pay- ments. This would be the di- rect consequence of a cover- up by certain operators who are deliberately concealing from the condition of agencies the certificating their North Sea hardware.
Or try it the other way. The oil industry is staffed by de- cent sensible people who know what they're playing at. Certainly lots of offshore in- stallations have developed lots of cracks but no one is the slightest bit surprised at this. Maintenance schedules are rigorous. Nothing is out of control.
Journalists are used to wrestling with conflicting ver- sions of events, but in Aber- deen the contrast between official and unofficial opinion is quite remarkable.

The Guardian 13th February 1981

You should now realize how important it is to select your words carefully when you are trying to persuade someone to accept your point of view. For further help with this form of writing, refer back to the chapter on *Argument* in Part A, pages 117–130.

Chapter Two

Punctuation

This chapter contains information about and exercises on:

Sentence markers: 1 The full stop

2 The exclamation mark

3 The question mark

Punctuation within the sentence: 1 The comma

2 The semi-colon

3 The colon

Punctuation for other purposes: 1 The apostrophe

2 Speech marks

3 The paragraph

Punctuation is an aid to reading written language. When we speak, we help our listeners understand what we are saying and how it fits together by using pauses and by making our voice pitch go up and down – rather like singing. Obviously, we cannot do this in writing so we have to find other ways, and to some extent, punctuation can be seen as the written equivalent of intonation. Indeed by listening to the pattern of your voice's movements up and down when you read your work, you can often get some idea of what the punctuation ought to be.

Punctuation marks perform two main functions.

a They *separate* units of language from one another. The units can be:

Units of the same kind which come one after another; for example, full stops are used to separate a sequence of sentences.

Units which are included in larger units; for example, commas are used to separate a word or group of words from the main part of the sentence.

b Some punctuation marks are used as signals that we have a particular language item; that is, they *specify* the kind of language unit. Examples of this kind are:

question marks
exclamation marks
apostrophes in words like *dog's collar*.

Sentence markers

1 The full stop

The full stop (.) is the punctuation mark which is used to show that a sentence has ended. If another sentence follows, then it should begin with a capital letter. For example:

> Shelley loved John. He did not love her.

However simple or however complicated the sentence, this rule must be followed. Here, for example, are some other sentences:

> After the party, the room was in a terrible mess.
> Get out of my way.
> I ran down the corridor, chased Mary round the corner, bumped into Amanda and collided with the Headmistress.

The full stop serves to mark that the sentence is completed.

Full stops are important since, if they are missed out, it can often be difficult to understand what is written. You will probably have to read this next example twice before you can make sense of it. Write it out with the full stops correctly inserted.

> I fell flat on my face while sitting on the ground and gathering my wits together I thought about how it had happened if I had not had that last drink I would never have been so clumsy it was my own fault

If you are in doubt about whether or not a full stop should be used then read your work out loud to yourself. You will be able to hear that your voice falls in pitch at certain points followed by a sense of starting again. This is often the place for a full stop. This should help tell you whether you have written a complete sentence and whether, therefore, you should use a full stop.

2 The exclamation mark

The exclamation mark (!) is used to mark the end of a sentence, and additionally to emphasize strong feelings such as surprise or shock or indignation. It is most appropriate for use in dialogue; elsewhere it is not usually suitable, except perhaps in informal personal letters.

The following examples demonstrate typical circumstances in which exclamation marks would be used in dialogue:

Ouch!	What a face!
Oh!	How stupid you are!
No! I'll never come.	I've never been so insulted!
Help!	Don't be silly!

Duplicating exclamation marks simply makes your writing look silly: one is always quite enough, however emphatic the statement. Neither is it a good idea to use too many exclamation marks in any one piece of writing. Save them for when they are really necessary.

3   The question mark

Whenever a sentence is couched in the form of a question, a question mark (?) is used. It marks the end of the sentence and gives us the additional information that the sentence is a question.

> What do you want?
> You will come, won't you?
> Is there any soup left?
> What is the difference between an elephant and a digital watch?

Notice that question marks are used even if the sentence in question form is not functioning as a real question:

> Will you please stop laughing?

Punctuation within the sentence

1   The comma

Full stops serve to indicate that a sentence has ended. Commas (,) are used *within* a sentence to show that there is a *small* break between one part of the sentence and another.

a) When there is a sequence of similar items in a sentence, commas are used to divide one from the next, in other words, to indicate a list. The items in the list can be single words:

> He boasted that he had O levels in Russian, Needlework, Biology, and English Literature.

or phrases:

> She looked for the cat in the garden, up the street, by the canal.

or clauses:

> She decided to stay at home because it was snowing, the car had no petrol in it, and there was a good film on the television.

Commas often (though not always) correspond to short pauses in speech. Try reading the sentences above without the breaks indicated by the commas and you may find yourself reading it as a breathless rush.

b) Commas are also used to signal an *inclusion* in a sentence. The included part may come at the beginning or end of the sentence, and may be a single word:

> Amazingly, I have never won the pools.

a phrase:

> On a wet Friday afternoon, the class was not at its brightest.

or a clause:

> Since he had just spent £35 on his new jacket, he was extremely annoyed when someone spilt beer all over it.

The included units may appear entirely within the larger units of the sentence. In this case they are separated from the rest of the sentence by commas. For example:

> The managing director arrived, finally, and the meeting began.

> His secretary, on the other hand, had been there for hours.

> The girl at the bus-stop, it seemed to him, was the most striking person he had ever seen.

In all these examples the commas indicate the relationship of the included part to the main part of the sentence.

c) There is one special use of commas to include a clause. In this case whether they are used or not makes an important difference to the meaning.

Look at these two sentences:

> John's brother who had been in India became a lumberjack.

> John's brother, who had been in India, became a lumberjack.

In the first sentence, the clause *who had been in India* tells you which of several possible brothers I am talking about. It narrows down the possible people that *John's brother* refers to.

In the second sentence, with commas:

> John's brother, who had been in India, became a lumberjack

we already knew who *John's brother* refers to, presumably because John only has one brother. Therefore the clause *who had been in India* does not restrict or narrow down the choices among possible brothers, instead it tells us more about the brother we already have in mind.

2   The semi-colon

The semi-colon (;) is used in two circumstances. Firstly, to separate the units in a list made up not of single words or phrases but of clauses:

> He was not the most attractive of men: spots sprouted over his face; his long, greasy hair dangled over his collar; a gingery beard grew half-heartedly out of his chin.

Secondly, when two closely connected but nevertheless separate statements are made within one sentence:

> I remember feeling in later life that no one else ever knew how *good* my father was; I doubt if even my mother knew.

> Iris Murdoch   *The Sea, The Sea*

In this example, it would have been possible to have separated these two statements by a full stop, but since the second statement develops the first Iris Murdoch has chosen to use a semi-colon rather than the full stop. It must, though, be emphasized that the decision whether or not to use a semi-colon in this kind of circumstance is very much a personal one. *If in doubt, use a full stop.* In the examples given, a full stop would not be wrong.

3   The colon

The colon (:) means roughly *as follows* in both its two main uses. Firstly it is used to introduce a list. For example:

> Since he liked to be well organized, he packed the following things for his night away: a toothbrush, a face flannel, pyjamas, soap, towel, hairbrush, clean socks and pants, and a peanut butter sandwich.

Secondly it is used when the second part of a sentence re-states or expands on an idea expressed in the first part:

> Above all there was the English examination: that was the most important thing in his life.

or

> His face loomed up in front of me: I saw a great, round blob of good intention.

The part which follows the colon (the re-statement or expansion) is usually a unit which could stand alone as a sentence, so again, it is often possible to use a full stop instead of a colon.

Punctuation for other purposes

1   The apostrophe

The apostrophe is a punctuation mark which acts as a signal for two kinds of language unit:

it indicates where part of a word has been left out in joining it to another word.

used before *s*, it is added to words to show *possession*.

a) In spoken language, we regularly use shortened forms of a number of words. The shortening is indicated in writing by replacing the letters not sounded with an apostrophe. Most writers do not use these contracted forms in writing except in dialogue, where they are quite usual. This is not a complete list but it gives the most common contracted forms. The words in the second column are shortened and added on to the words in the first; the letters added on are underlined; the letters omitted and replaced by an apostrophe are *not* underlined.

he, she, it		he's, she's, it's
there, here, where	+ is	— there's, here's, where's
we, you, they	+ are	— we're, you're, they're
I, we, you, they	+ have	— I've, we've, you've, they've
he, she, it, there	+ has	— he's, she's, it's, there's

I, you, she, etc.	+ had	– I'd, you'd, she'd, etc.
	+ would	–
I, you, he, etc.	+ will	– I'll, you'll, he'll, etc.
do, did		don't, didn't
has, have,	+ not	hasn't, haven't
is, are, etc.		isn't, aren't, etc.

The only exceptions to this pattern are:

can	+ not	– can't
will	+ not	– won't

b) When we add s to nouns to show possession we use an apostrophe before the s in writing.

> Jane's mother
> A chef's hat
> A dog's dinner
> The baby's rattle.

Notice that some possessive pronouns end in -s but, perhaps surprisingly, they do not have an apostrophe. The rules about 's apply only to nouns.

> yours, his, hers, its, ours, theirs.

In English we add -s to words for two other reasons besides indicating possession; -s has two other functions in grammar:

i) to show plurals

> a pen – several pens.

ii) to mark the third person singular in the present tense of verbs:

> I speak
> you speak
> he, she speaks.

-s for possession is distinguished from these two uses in writing by the use of the apostrophe. *It is only when -s indicates possession that an apostrophe is used.*

-s plural and -s in verbs do *not* have apostrophes.

When a possessive noun already has an -s on it to show plural, the possession is shown simply by adding an apostrophe. Only one grammatical -s can be added to a word, and plural -s takes precedence. Thus:

several teachers	– several teachers' cars
these girls	– these girls' clothes.

172

2 Speech marks

Speech marks (or quotation marks as they are sometimes called) are used to indicate the words which are actually spoken by someone. In printed books you will see both single and double quotation marks, but in handwriting double marks are normally used.

'You're an idiot, John,' Shelley said.

Here the words *'You're an idiot, John'* are what Shelley said so they are enclosed in speech marks. Exactly the same rule holds if the words which are spoken come *after* the speaker's name.

Shelley said, 'You're an idiot, John.'

Note the following points:

a) Whether *Shelley said* comes after or before the words which she speaks, the first word which is spoken must have a capital letter.

'You're an idiot, John,' Shelley said.
Shelley said, 'You're an idiot, John.'

b) This rule does *not* hold when the sentence which is being spoken is interrupted by the speaker's name and the verb:

'You're an idiot, John,' Shelley said, 'but I like you all the same.'

The word 'but' which begins the second part of what is said does not need a capital letter because it is *the same sentence* which continues after the interruption of *Shelley said*.

If, however, a new sentence is begun after the speaker's name and the verb, then a capital letter is needed:

'You're an idiot, John,' Shelley said. 'It seems you take after your father.'

Note, too, that a full stop is needed after *Shelley said* rather than a comma. This is because the first sentence has ended and a new one is to begin.

c) Punctuation marks are always placed *inside* the speech marks:

'It is raining outside,' she said.
'Help me!' I cried.
'What do you want?' he said.

It does not matter whether it is a comma, an exclamation mark or a question mark: the punctuation mark is always placed inside the speech marks. In this case the exclamation mark and the question mark are not marking the end of a sentence; instead they are performing their other function of specifying the kind of unit it is: an exclamation or a question.

d) When two or more people are speaking, it is usual to begin a new paragraph each time a new speaker begins to talk. This point is demonstrated in the following passage. Note also from this passage that it is not always necessary to write 'he said' or 'she said' at the end of each sentence spoken. Once the pattern of the speech becomes clear, the reader can understand what is happening without these reminders.

> His daughter looked at him and her eyebrows went up in tired forbearance.
>   'Put your birds to bed?' she asked, humouring him.
>   'Lucy,' he said urgently. 'Lucy . . .'
>   'Well what is it now?'
>   'She's in the garden with Steven.'
>   'Now you just sit down and have your tea.'

e) Quotation marks are also used for the following purposes:

  i) to quote an extract from a piece of writing. For example:
  In paragraph three the author refers to 'the piton stance'.

 ii) to mark the title of a book or film, the name of a ship, or a nickname. For example:
  'Have you been to see "Casablanca" yet?'

iii) to indicate a word used in an unusual sense. For example:
  Some schools operate a system of 'family grouping'.

The paragraph

In order to make it easier for readers to follow the stages of an argument or the development of a story, almost every piece of writing of any length is divided into paragraphs. Each new paragraph should, therefore, signify that one group of ideas has ended and that a new group is beginning. The fact that each new paragraph begins on a new line and is indented an inch or two serves to indicate visually to the reader that this is happening.* In the following passage, for example, you will see that each paragraph develops a particular point. When the writer has said all that he wishes to say on one point, he starts a new paragraph and embarks on the next stage of his argument. This makes the argument clearer and more force-ful.

> The social importance of sport has never been more apparent than it is today. Yet rarely has its need been less understood, and its provision less adequate.
>   The ingredients of disaster exist in all Britain's cities, includ-ing urban stress and deprivation. The recent events in Bristol show the price of neglect. Fundamental to any understanding of present problems – whether these be football hooliganism, com-munity disturbance or neighbourhood vandalism – is the need for an appreciation of the importance of good influences in the lives of youngsters.
>   The family is the bedrock of civilized society, but it is the last consideration in the minds of administrators when providing for education. The truth is that the education of parents in family

responsibility is non-existent in most areas.

In so many homes the wife has been expected to go out to work, to return and clean the house, to cook for the family and to find her only relaxation in putting up her feet, watching the box, and discouraging all conversation. At a time when communication between the generations was never more important, it has never been more lacking. As for providing sport and recreation opportunities for women, that is still the biggest area of neglect by both our local authorities and our sports bodies.

The schools do a wonderful job in school time, but no representative of authority calls, since rent collectors have been abolished in the name of economy, playing fields are poor, sports equipment non-existent. So vandalism flourishes, and out of this environment emerges the unemployed youngster, frustrated and disillusioned, seeking a collective identity, since the means of developing an individual personality are so hard to come by.

Sport has more to offer in terms of combating boredom, the root cause of so many of these problems, then almost any other social activity. It also holds out better prospects of producing good community relationships than most other investments. Yet the small allocation of resources which was provided when I was the responsible Minister has not even been matched by the present Government, much less extended.

Denis Howell *The Times Educational Supplement* 3.10.80

*You will find more information about organizing your material within each paragraph on page 145.

☐ There are six paragraphs in this passage. What idea does each paragraph focus upon?

☐ Descriptive essays also benefit from careful division into paragraphs. Read, for example, the next piece of writing. In the first paragraph the writer describes a farm and its setting. He then focusses upon the jackdaws and the carter's boy in the second paragraph, and the fox in the third. What is said in the last paragraph which makes it different from the previous descriptive paragraphs?

January

It is January, and the predominant grass is green and shining in the sun. The rusty oaks and the farmhouse roofs glow. The bare clean hedges glitter with all their stems of olive hazel, silver oak and ash and whitethorn, and blackthorn ruddy where the cattle have rubbed. A lark rises and sings. A flock of linnets scatters and drops little notes like a rain of singing dew, and over all is a high blue sky, across which the west wind sets a fleet of bright white

175

clouds to sail: into this blue sky the woods of the horizon drive their black teeth.

In the immense crystal spaces of fine windy air thus bounded by blue sky, black woods, and green grass, the jackdaws play. They soar, they float, they dance, and they dive and carve sudden magnificent precipices in the air, crying all the time with sharp, joyous cries that are in harmony with the great heights and the dashing wind. The carter's boy raises his head from the furrow and shouts to them now and then, while the brass furnishings of his horses gleam, their shoulders grow proud and their black tails stream out above the blue furrow and the silver plough.

Suddenly a pheasant is hurled out of a neighbouring copse; something crosses the road; and out over a large and shining meadow goes a fox, tall and red, going easily as if he sailed in the wind. He crosses that meadow, then another, and he is half a mile away before a loud halloo sounds in the third field, and a mile away before the first hound crosses the road upon his scent.

Run hard, hounds, and drown the jackdaws' calling with your concerted voices. It is good to see your long swift train across the meadow and away, away; on such a day a man would give everything to run like that. Run hard, fox, and may you escape, for it would not be well to die on such a day, unless you could perchance first set your fair teeth into the throats of the foolish ones who now break through the hedge on great horses and pursue you – I know not why – ignorant of the command that has gone forth from the heart of this high blue heaven, Be beautiful and enjoy and live!

Ed. Roland Gant   *Edward Thomas on the Countryside*

Exercises

Full stops and commas

☐ Punctuate the following passages correctly. Full stops, capital letters and commas need to be inserted.

1 in the evening he arrived in the region of weimar he came upon sentries who challenged him in german he was shot at he ran headlong into the night until he felt as if his head lungs and heart would burst and that a clot of blood was lodged in his throat

2 muriel obeyed and sabine left the room followed by her son and daughter the latter turning to cast a cold appraising glance behind as though with some private purpose

3 walking in winter brings its own delights in this modern world one of these is the ability to enjoy a quietness so often absent in popular countryside in summer it must be hard for the town dweller particularly the

young town dweller to realize the true significance of darkness it is nowadays difficult to experience true and total darkness in our land but here and there now and then we may recall the true darkness of winter known long ago before towns were so extensive and so well illuminated at night in most parts of the peak district for instance it is difficult to find a really black night environment even on the wilder moorland tops the orange glow of manchester and sheffield diffuses into the sky and kills the illusion of the wilderness

4 soon after the dance is over the navajo begin to ride down the western trail into the light their women with velvet bodices and full skirts silver and turquoise tinkling thick on their breasts sit back on their horses and ride down the steep slope looking wonderingly around from their pleasant broad nomadic mongolian faces

5 they were on top of the world now it was naked too as the back of your fist high under heaven and dull heavy green only it was veined with a network of old stone walls dividing the fields and broken here and there with ruins of old lead mines and works a sparse stone farm bristled with six naked sharp trees in the distance was a patch of smoky grey stone a hamlet in some fields grey dark sheep fed silently sombrely but there was not a sound nor a movement it was the roof of england stony and arid as any roof beyond below were the shires

6 we had provided the snakes with a hollow log as a home and both were inside with only their heads showing each head shaped like the club pip on a playing card the rat ran around and then passed too close to the log suddenly one of the snakes moved like a flicker of light he struck the rat and returned to position so fast his coils seemed barely to twitch the rat went straight up in the air when he came down he ran wildly for a few seconds then fell on his side twitching spasmodically he was dead in less than a quarter of a minute

☐ Decide whether or not the following sentences should have commas round the words in italics, in the light of the information you are given. Write the sentences out correctly punctuated.

1 Would you pass me the book *which is next to the rubber plant*?
(There are books next to the rubber plant, on the table and on the floor.)

2 My friends *who live in Bristol* are coming for the weekend.
(These friends are the only friends I have.)

3 The question *which Mr Smith raised* is a very interesting one.
(Questions have been raised by Mr Smith, Ms Brown and Lady de Vere.)

4 I ate the cake *which was covered in cream*.
(It was the last cake on the plate.)

5 My teacher was a woman *who knew her own mind*.
(You already know my teacher was a woman.)

6 The tomato sauce is in the cupboard *where the marmalade is kept*.
(There is one cupboard.)

7 You will find the table mats in the drawer *where the cutlery is*. (There are three drawers.)

8 Sarah *who is a lorry driver* still managed to fall off her bicycle. (You did not know Sarah's job.)

Question marks and exclamation marks

Question marks and exclamation marks have been left out of the following sentences. Punctuate the sentences correctly.

1 What on earth do you think you are doing

2 There is just no excuse for your behaviour

3 It is hardly fair You want me to pay for everything, don't you

4 However, to repeat Lizzie's own perfectly reasonable question, what do I want Oh why do women take everything so intensely seriously and make such a fuss Why do they always demand definitions, explanations

5 What's the matter You aren't hurt, are you David Answer me Please why don't you speak

The semi-colon

Commas and semi-colons have been left out of the following sentences. Punctuate the sentences correctly.

1 I shall do that shortly for the moment the exchanges are continuing.

2 I did not know I did not know what I did.

3 It was terrible weather: the wind blew ceaselessly each night the temperature dropped below freezing the rain fell vertically.

4 He had a sudden perception of the strange hazardousness of existence of how little a word from her a raised phone it would have taken for such a meeting to have been.

5 It was impossible to regard her as a perfectly well-conducted young lady she was wanting in a certain indispensable delicacy.

6 Lovingly he revisited the handsome men at croquet handsome men at war disdainful boys in boaters girls at Cheltenham a whole long history of discomfort and not a breath of passion.

7 He walked slowly down the street his hand turned the letter over and over in his pocket.

8 He pushed the table away from the window and lifted the suitcase with the key from the chain he unlocked it praying all the time that nothing was broken from the journey.

9 They were talking a great deal they had not seen each other for a long time.

10 The rest of the group were ready to go the women were looking for their coats the men were standing together just outside the door.

The colon

Commas, semi-colons and colons have been left out of the following sentences. Punctuate the sentences correctly.

1 It was Amanda who saw him first a tall thin figure standing on his own on the edge of the platform.
2 He wanted little out of life a house of some sort enough money to buy food and drink a few friends that he might see occasionally.
3 By way of emphasis the western side is adorned with the grotesque statuary of political impotence a plywood model of the Brandenburg gate the screws rusting in their sockets rises absurdly from an untended field notice boards broken by wind and rain display fifteen-year-old slogans across an empty valley.
4 He looked round the room and they were all there Sarah with her long brown hair looking slightly ill at ease Michael squinting suspiciously from the sofa Jonathan running his fingers through his greasy hair.
5 At that moment he knew that there was no hope they had found the letter.
6 The walls were filled with pictures of some unknown family sketches in sepia miniatures photographs faded with age.
7 The assorted junk he was taking with him stood on the station platform an old bicycle various tatty cases a violin in a greasy battered case a pile of paperbacks tied hopefully together with string.
8 It was shiny and attractive mechanically perfect beautifully upholstered a bargain.
9 The red letters were just decipherable on the wooden board Danger from falling rocks.
10 Thus the first day ended setting the pattern for those that followed carefree exciting days for both of them days of honest labour and cautious but deepening attachment as the skills of boyhood became once more the weapons of war.

Apostrophes

Add apostrophes where appropriate in the following sentences.

1 If shes looking for bargains shell certainly get her moneys worth.
2 Id rather he didnt throw away Julies books.
3 Two policemens helmets were found on New Years Eve; their owners havent claimed them yet.
4 The childrens grandfather takes them for long walks every week.
5 Youre to make sure the twins keep out of harms way.
6 An elephants memory lasts forever.
7 The burglars story wasnt convincing enough for the detectives.
8 Im taking a weeks holiday in a months time; I'll probably go to the Channel Islands.

Speech marks

Punctuate the following passages correctly.

1 oh no said the boy casually i won't think much about them mother you needn't worry i wouldn't worry mother if i were you
    if you were me and i were you said his mother i wonder what we should do
    but you know you needn't worry mother don't you the boy repeated
    i should be awfully glad to know it she said wearily
    oh well you can you know i mean you ought to know you needn't worry he insisted
    ought i then i'll see about it she said

2 the next day mayo said you found it
    right said hood ask murf
    i don't know nothing said murf
    but you know we found it don't you squire
    oh yeah i know that said murf but i don't know nothing else
    so that's why you wanted the van i leave the house for six hours and i come back to a muddle give me the keys
    hood handed her the keys and said there's no muddle sweetheart everything's fine we found the stuff now stop shouting
    i think you're lying said mayo

3 who are you i asked in a faint voice
    i'm the hotel nurse
    what's the matter with me
    poisoned she said briefly poisoned the whole lot of you i never seen anythin' like it sick here sick there whatever you young ladies been stuffin' yourselves with
    is everybody else sick too i asked with some hope
    the whole lot of you she affirmed with relish sick as dogs and cryin' for ma

Chapter Three

Spelling

It is often said that English spelling is illogical and random and unsystematic, because we don't spell words the way we say them. People point to words like:

thought   though   cough   bough   through

to show that the same letters can be pronounced in several different ways.

There is, however, more pattern and regularity in English spelling than many people think, and if you are alert to these patterns you are less likely to make mistakes in your spelling.

English spelling is not 'phonetic' in the way that, for example, Spanish spelling is. That is to say, the letters are not always pronounced in the same way, and the sounds may be spelt with different letters. One reason is that there are 44 sounds in English but only 26 letters. There are other reasons, some of which will be suggested below. They have to do with the fact that spelling is a *visual* system, designed to give the reader other kinds of information which will help him or her understand the text: information about grammar, about relationships among words and differences between them for example. This information may be more useful than information about how a word is pronounced, and it can be represented in spelling in a systematic way. There *are* patterns in spelling which can help writer as well as reader, and a writer whose eye recognizes these patterns will be a better speller.

What, then, can spelling do?

1 First we can use spelling as a way of differentiating between words which sound the same. These may be completely different words:

rough	ruff
scene	seen
bough	bow
altar	alter
stationary	stationery etc.

Or they may be related words which have different grammatical functions: some of these sound slightly different too:

licence (n)	license (v)	wreath (n)	wreathe (v)
practice (n)	practise (v)	bath (n)	bathe (v)
advice (n)	advise (v)	smooth (a)	smoothe (v) etc.
breath (n)	breathe (v)		

181

Or they may be words which came to be used as personal names, and we use the spelling to keep them separate from the non-name words:

car	Carr
toy	Toye
man	Mann
moor	Moore	etc.

Here, we are using the *visual* resources of the written language to make distinctions and help sort out possible confusions. Word-pairs which sound the same but are spelt differently are much more common in English than words which look the same but sound different:

read   lead   etc.

2 Secondly, English makes use of the fact that spelling is a visual system to distinguish between 'full' words with a proper dictionary meaning and 'grammatical' words which we use to stick the bits of a sentence together. For example, almost all one and two letter words in English are grammatical words (the only common exception is *ox*) and similar-sounding 'full' words are spelt with three letters:

I	eye
be	bee
up	
at	
in	inn
us	
as	ass
by	buy
so	sow
no	know
to	two	etc.

In this way in a piece of continuous writing the reader's eye is helped in finding a way through the text by being able to recognize and distinguish the 'grammar' words which help us to understand the structure of the sentence.

3 Thirdly, the spelling system of English preserves regularity in the spelling of words which are related to one another even if they sound different in speech. This can help you learn to spell a number of words, because you can relate them to words you already know. The sounds of the words you know can help you remember how to spell words related to them. This is much less confusing than trying to learn spellings from lists of words which are spelt similarly. In this list the pronunciation of the words in the first column can help you to spell the words in the second.

suspect	suspicion
effect	efficient

medical	medicine
existential	existence
signal	sign
differential	different
grammatical	grammar
precede	precedence
science	conscience
relate	relative
metallic	metal
editorial	editor
hilarity	exhilarating
ease	disease (dis-ease)
finite	definite

This generalization, that the spelling preserves the regularity of related words, applies also to parts of words. To give two simple examples, the past tense of regular verbs in English is pronounced in three ways – d, t, and id – but it is spelled – ed:

pronounced d – loved, cared, banned
pronounced t – hissed, laughed, banked
pronounced id – hated, painted, polluted.

Again, the plural of most nouns is spelt with an -s but this too represents three different pronunciations.

pronounced s – cats, ducks
pronounced z – dogs, cows, hens
pronounced iz – horses, matches

4 Fourthly, our spelling system has different rules for different parts of words – such as the beginning, the middle, and the end. It probably helps to think of a number of different sub-systems of spelling, each with its own rules. Again, this actually helps us to read as we become used to the patterns we can expect. For instance, take the sound f. This can be spelt in a number of ways, but we can't choose which way at random.

It can be spelt f at the beginnings of words:

fun, fume, food, foot …

It can be spelt f before t:

rift, shaft, rafter …

It can be spelt ff in the middle and at the ends of words:

puffer, muffler, scuffle …
scuff, huff, riff, stiff …

It can be spelt ph in words borrowed from Greek, and mostly in certain units which recur:

    phil-   : philosophy, philanthropy, anglophili ...
    phobe- : phobia, claustrophobic ...
    phone- : gramophone, telephone, phonetic ...
    graph- : telegraph, graphic ...

It can be spelt -gh at the ends of words and before t in the groups ough or augh.

    cough   laugh
    draught   enough

Try writing similar sets of rules for the sounds sh, ch, (in church) j.

The letter e

Many spelling mistakes arise from problems with this letter. It has some special functions in our spelling system and if writers understood these and were able to see them as aspects of the same thing, many errors would be avoided. The letter e functions as a 'dummy' letter at the ends of words in a number of related ways.

i) It is a signal that the preceding vowel is pronounced as a long vowel or diphthong and not as a simple short vowel.

    Compare:

        hat   hate
        met   mete
        sit   site
        dot   dote
        jut   jute

ii) Our spelling system has a rule which says that words cannot end in certain letters (unless, say, they are borrowed from another language). So e comes at the ends of words which would otherwise end in these letters:

    -i   tie, lie, die
    -u   sue, cue, rue
    -v   live, love, leave
    -z   freeze, sneeze

iii) When a word ends in j sound, this sound is represented by the group of letters -dge or -age.

    hedge, judge, ridge   etc.
    courage, damage   etc.

iv) Words which end in an s sound have e added to them because otherwise they would look as though they were plurals – and we have already seen how important it is to consider the effect of patterns of spelling on the reader's eye.

    horse, house, mouse, chase   etc.

v) The letter e also forms part of a number of suffixes:

-es	halves, passes, batches
-en	flatten, soften, spoken, children
-er	singer, fighter, bigger, paler
-est	flattest, softest, biggest, palest
-ed	jumped, smoked, failed.

Notice that in all these examples, there is no e sound like the one in *egg*, for example. The fact that they all use e is part of the systematic pattern of spelling, and again, is a help to the reader's eye.

A note on suffixes

Examples (i)–(iv) above have something in common: when other bits – suffixes – are added on to the words which use them, the e is no longer needed, and is left off. Thus:

hate	hating (+ing)
dote	doting
tie	tying (notice the i becomes y, because the system won't allow ii)
sue	suing
live	living
freeze	freezing
judge	judging
house	housing

This rule also applies to many other suffixes which begin with a vowel, e.g.: -ive, -able, -ible, -ity, -ence   etc.

Notice that we can say the same about the suffixes beginning with (v) above – they begin with a vowel too, so when they are added to words ending in e, the final e in the original word is left off, and the e in the spelling is part of the suffix. Thus it fits in with our suffix spelling pattern to think of the following words as having this arrangement:

hate	hat – ing
	hat – er
	hat – ed (not hate – d)

There is another important spelling rule which affects what happens when we add suffixes to words. We have seen that the special functions of e at the ends of words in group (i) (ii) (iii) and (iv) above can also be performed by vowels in suffixes. Therefore in words which *don't* have a dummy -e, e.g. *dot* the spelling has to show that the sound stays the same when suffixes are added. It does this by doubling the consonants at the ends of words. Thus:

	dote	doting
but	dot	dotting

185

We can describe all the rules for dropping -e and for doubling consonants in the same way. They are rules for making sure that the spelling continues to represent the vowel sound of the word when suffixes are added to it.

Remember that all this only applies to suffixes beginning with a vowel. For those beginning with a consonant, the jobs performed by dummy -e are still important, and the e still appears in the spelling:

-ly   sincerely, rudely
-ful   careful, plateful
-ness   ripeness, paleness

George Bernard Shaw once suggested that the word *fish* could be spelt 'ghoti'

gh = f as in *enough*
o = i as in *women*
ti = sh as in *station*

We can now see why no English speaker would ever pronounce 'ghoti' as *fish*. We all know and follow certain rules of spelling and pronunciation which make it impossible.

> Gh at the beginnings of words is always pronounced g, as in *ghost*. List all the words you can think of beginning with gh. Do they have anything in common besides their spelling? As we have seen above, gh can only be pronounced as f in the groups -ough(t) and -aught(t), as in *cough, laugh*.
>
> O is only pronounced i in the word *women*, to preserve its similarity and connection with the singular *woman*, and to avoid the difficulties that would arise in reading the handwritten version of 'wimin', (try it!)
>
> ti is pronounced sh only in the suffixes -tion -tious, which are treated in spelling as related units, so their spelling is constant and similar. We can't treat the ti of -tion separately from the other letters in the unit as they might be in *tin, fetid, stingy*, for example.

Once we are aware of the regular patterns and rules that govern English spelling, we can see that it is not as irrational as many people think. It is designed for the eye, and for the eye of someone who knows the language (as you do). It is not a 'phonetic' system – that is, there is not always a clear and regular link between sound and spelling – but we can be glad that it is not, because the spelling can help us in other ways than simply telling us how a word is pronounced. Since it is a system designed for the eye, as a writer you need to bear that in mind and develop an alertness to the look of words.

Acknowledgements

The author and publisher wish to thank the following for permission to use extracts from copyright material:

Al Alvarez: from *Hard Rock* (edited by Ken Wilson). Reprinted by permission of Granada Publishing Ltd.

Michael Anthony: from *Drunkard of the River*. Reprinted by permission of Andre Deutsch Ltd.

John Berger: from *A Fortunate Man* (Allen Lane 1967).

Keith Bosley: "I have watched the street it stood in . . ." extract from 'No. 14'. Copyright © 1979 Keith Bosley. By permission of the author (p. 39).

Malcolm Bradbury: from *The History Man*. Reprinted by permission of Martin Secker & Warburg Ltd.

Margaret Drabble: From *The Needle's Eye* and *The Realms of Gold*. Reprinted by permission of Weidenfeld (Publishers) Ltd.

Douglas Dunn: 'Late night walk down Terry Street' from *Terry Street*. Reprinted by permission of Faber & Faber Ltd.

T. S. Eliot: 'Preludes I' from *Collected Poems 1909–1962*. Reprinted by permission of Faber & Faber Ltd.

Ian Fleming: from *Goldfinger*. Reprinted by permission of Jonathan Cape Ltd., for the author and Glidrose Productions.

Frederick Forsyth: from *The Day of the Jackal* (Hutchinson 1971).

Gallup Poll. for tables from national survey on attitudes to disabled. First published in *New Society*. (See pp. 115–116.)

Roland Gant: from *Edward Thomas on the Countryside* (edited by R. Gant). Reprinted by permission of Faber & Faber Ltd.

Alan Garner: from *Red Shift*. Reprinted by permission of Collins Publishers.

Stuart Hall: 'Crossroads Nowhere' in *West Indian Stories* (edited by A. Salkey, Faber 1960).

Seamus Heaney: 'Boy Driving His Father to Confession' was originally published by Martin Booth (Sceptre Press). Reprinted by permission of the author.

John Hedgecoe: from *John Hedgecoe's Introductory Photography Course*. Reprinted by permission of Mitchell Beazley International Ltd.

Susan Hill: from *The Bird of Night* and *In The Springtime of the Year*. Reprinted by permission of Hamish Hamilton Ltd.

Richard Hoggart: from *The Uses of Literacy*. Reprinted by permission of the author and Chatto & Windus Ltd.

James Joyce: from 'The Boarding House' from *Dubliners*. Reprinted by permission of the Executors of the James Joyce Estate and Jonathan Cape Ltd.

John Le Carre: from *The Looking Glass War*. Reprinted by permission of William Heinemann Ltd.

London, Your Sightseeing Guide, 1979. Extract reprinted by permission of the British Tourist Authority.

Macmillan Family Encyclopedia. Copyright Arete Publishing Company Inc., 1980. By permission.

Shiva Naipaul: from *The Chip-Chip Gatherers*. Reprinted by permission of André Deutsch Ltd.

New Society. Extracts from The Hidden Army, *New Society*, 20.12.79. By permission. (See page 90.)

The Observer. Extract reprinted by permission of the Observer News Service, London.

George Orwell: from *The Road to Wigan Pier, Boys' Weeklies* and *Shooting An Elephant*. Reprinted by permission of A. M. Heath & Co. Ltd., for the estate of the late George Orwell and for the publisher, Martin Secker & Warburg Ltd.

The Oxford Star. Extracts reprinted by permission of the Editor.

Boris Pasternak: from *Doctor Zhivago*. Reprinted by permission of Collins Publishers.

Jonathan Raban: from *Soft City*. Reprinted by permission of Gillon Aitken.

The Sunday Times. Extracts reprinted by permission of The Sunday Times, London (Syndication Dept.).

Paul Theroux: from *The Family Arsenal*. Reprinted by permission of Gillon Aitken.

The Times Educational Supplement. Extracts reprinted by permission of Times Newspapers Ltd.

H. F. Wallis: from *The New Battle of Britain* (Charles Knight 1972).

Richard Wright: from *Black Boy* Reprinted by permission of Mrs. Ellen Wright and Jonathan Cape Ltd.

Acknowledgement is also due to the following exam boards for permission to reprint questions from past English papers:

The Associated Examining Board, Aldershot, Hants.

Associated Lancashire Schools Examining Board, Manchester.

Joint Matriculation Board, Manchester.

London Regional Examining Board (formerly Metropolitan Regional Examinations Board).

Oxford and Cambridge Schools Examination Board, Cambridge.

Welsh Joint Education Committee, Cardiff.

The publishers have made every effort to trace and contact copyright holders, but in some cases without success, and apologise for any infringement of copyright.

Index of authors and titles of works quoted

The publishers would like to thank the following for permission to reproduce photographs:

Aerofilms pp. 6, 26; Simon Bran p. 27; Camera Press p. 124; Hunter Cordaiy p. 9; Robin Crofts p. 7; Fine Fare Limited p. 13; Martine Franck from The John Hillelson Agency p. 9; Richard and Sally Greenhill pp. 45, 48, 54, 55; Nick Hedges p. 63; Preparatory Study of Mr. Clark, drawing by David Hockney courtesy Petersburg Press p. 43; Raven Accessories p. 12; Tate Gallery pp. 42, 43; Peter Town p. 45